SPEECHES

IN THE

SECOND AND THIRD SESSIONS

OF THE

THIRTY-SEVENTH CONGRESS,

AND IN THE VACATION.

BY BENJ. F. THOMAS.

BOSTON:
PRINTED BY JOHN WILSON AND SON.
1863.

To my Brother,

WILLIAM THOMAS, ESQ.,

This Volume is Inscribed,

AS A TOKEN OF ESTEEM, LOVE, AND GRATITUDE.

"*I set out with a perfect distrust of my own abilities; a total renunciation of every speculation of my own; and with a profound reverence for the wisdom of our ancestors, who have left us the inheritance of so happy a constitution, and so flourishing an empire, and, what is a thousand times more valuable, the treasury of the maxims and principles which formed the one, and obtained the other.*"

BURKE on Conciliation with America.

NOTE.

The speeches and addresses in this volume cover a period of about fifteen months, including the second and third sessions of the Thirty-seventh Congress and the vacation. I have put them in this form to meet the wishes of a few friends, in justice to myself, — that my position may not be misunderstood — and in the hope, not very buoyant, that they may do good. I am painfully sensible how fragmentary and defective they are. But the principles they seek to illustrate and defend are just and true, and will weather the storm. They constitute the traditional policy of the country, a return to which is, in my judgment, its only security. That they are unpopular at this moment, does not disturb me: the more imperative is the duty of standing by and upholding them. The citizen owes to the country, in the hour of her peril, honest counsel, calmly given, but with the "love that casteth out fear." Never were freedom of thought and of the lips and pen so necessary as now. They have become, not only the most precious of rights, but the most religious of duties.

In preparing for the printer, I have corrected a few of the errors of style. I have not felt at liberty to make material changes in the thought. In one or two instances (as in the remarks on the Conscription Bill), I have added, from notes, suggestions omitted at the time of delivery. The recurrence of the same idea, and of even the same expression, in different speeches on the same or kindred topics, could not well be avoided.

From the remarks on the Trent case, I have stricken two or three sentences which were thought to breathe a spirit of vengeance; a spirit the gospel does not permit us to indulge, even against the enemies of our country. Of the expressions of confidence in the conservative views of the President, I can only say, I believed them well grounded when they were made.

JAMAICA PLAIN, May 25, 1863.

CONTENTS.

	Page.
THE RELATION OF THE "SECEDED STATES" (SO CALLED) TO THE UNION, AND THE CONFISCATION OF PROPERTY, AND EMANCIPATION OF SLAVES, IN SUCH STATES	1
CONFISCATION	38
THE TREASURY-NOTE BILL	66
RECOGNITION OF LIBERIA AND HAYTI	79
DEATH OF HON. GOLDSMITH F. BAILEY	86
CASE OF THE "TRENT"	91
SPEECH AT THE MASS MEETING FOR RECRUITING, ON BOSTON COMMON	100
THE ARMY OF THE RESERVE	104
SPEECH AT CHELSEA	128
REMARKS ON THE BORDER STATES	141
ON THE BILL "TO RAISE ADDITIONAL SOLDIERS FOR THE SERVICE OF THE GOVERNMENT"	145
THE LOUISIANA ELECTION CASES	164
THE CONSCRIPTION BILL	184
NEW ENGLAND AND THE UNION	193

SPEECHES.

THE RELATION OF THE "SECEDED STATES" (SO CALLED) TO THE UNION, AND THE CONFISCATION OF PROPERTY, AND EMANCIPATION OF SLAVES, IN SUCH STATES, APRIL 10, 1862.

The House being in Committee of the Whole on the State of the Union, Mr. THOMAS said, —

Mr. CHAIRMAN, — I avail myself of the indulgence of the Committee to make some suggestions upon subjects now attracting the attention of Congress and of the country, — the relations of the "seceded States" (so called) to the Union, the confiscation of property, and the emancipation of slaves, in such States. Sensible how deeply the interests of the country are involved in their right decision, I can only say, I have given to them careful and patient consideration, with an earnest hope and desire to learn what my duty is, and faithfully and firmly to discharge it.

The questions are novel as they are momentous. In the discussion of them, little aid can be derived from our own precedents, from the history of other nations, or from writers on constitutional and international law. The solution of the difficult problems of right and duty involved must be found in the careful study of the principles of the Constitution, and the just and logical application of them to this new condition of things.

The peculiar feature of our civil polity is, that we live under written constitutions, defining and limiting the powers of Government, and securing the rights of the individual subject. Our political theory is, that the people retain the sovereignty, and that the Government has such powers only as the people, by the organic law, have conferred upon it. Doubless these inflexible rules sometimes operate as a restraint upon measures, which, for the time being, seem to be desirable. The compensation is, that our experience has shown, that, as a general rule and in the long-run, the restraint is necessary and wholesome.

It is, I readily admit, by no narrow and rigid construction of the words of the Constitution that the powers and duties of Congress on these subjects are to be ascertained. Every provision must be fairly construed in view of the great objects the Constitution was ordained to effect, and with the full recognition of the powers resulting from clear implication as well as express grant. Designed as the bond of perpetual union and as the framework of permanent government, we should be very slow to conclude that it lacked any of the necessary powers for self-defence and self-preservation.

But recognizing the profound wisdom and foresight of the Constitution, and its adaptation to all the exigencies of war and peace, when a measure is proposed in apparent conflict with its provisions, we may well pause to inquire, whether, after all, the measure *is* necessary; and whether we may not bend to the Constitution, rather than that the Constitution should give way to us. When we make necessity our lawgiver, we are very ready to believe the necessity exists.

Nor are we to forget that the Constitution is a bill of rights as well as a frame of government; that among the most precious portions of the instrument are the first ten amendments; that it is doubtful whether the people of the United States could have been induced to adopt the Constitution, except upon the assurance of the adoption of these amendments, which are our Magna Carta, embodying in the organic law the securities of life, liberty, and estate, which, to the Anglo-Saxon mind, are the seed and the fruit of free government. Some portions of our history have led to the conclusion, that the existence of these amendments may, in the confusion of the times, have been overlooked.

In my humble judgment, Mr. Chairman, there has been, and is now, but one issue before the country; and that is, whether the Constitution of the United States shall be the supreme law of the land. That Constitution was formed by the *people* of the United States. It acts, not upon the States, nor, through the States, upon us as citizens of the several States, but directly upon us as citizens of the United States; claiming, on the one hand, our allegiance, and giving to us, on the other, its protection. It is not a compact between the States, or the peoples of the several States: it is itself a frame of government ordained and established by the people of the United States.

The sphere of the Government so established is indeed limited; but within that sphere its power is supreme. It is a Government of delegated powers; and the powers not delegated are reserved either to the States or to the people (Amendments, art. 10).

The powers and functions granted to the National Government by the Constitution are embraced in three general classes, — those concerning the relations of the United States to foreign nations; those concerning the relations between the States and their citizens respectively; and certain powers, which, though belonging to the home-department of Government, to be useful and effective, must be general and uniform in their operation throughout the country. A very large proportion of the ordinary and necessary powers and functions of Government is left in the States. The powers of the National Government do not extend to or include the domestic institutions or internal police of the States. The separation and distinction between the respective spheres of the State and National Governments is an essential characteristic of our system, and is as old as the idea of Union itself. No Union was suggested, no project of one for a moment entertained, on any other basis. The Colonies, in authorizing their delegates to assent to a separation from Great Britain, and to form a Union for the general defence, expressly restricted them from consenting to any articles of union which should take from the Colonies the power over their internal police and domestic institutions. The resolutions of the Colonies of New Jersey, Maryland, and Rhode Island, may be cited in illustration.

The resolution of the Provincial Congress of New Jersey — passed June 21, 1776, and laid before the Continental Congress on the 28th of June — empowered the delegates of that Province to —

"Unite with the delegates of the other Colonies in declaring the United Colonies independent of Great Britain; entering into a confederation for union and common defence; making treaties with foreign nations for commerce and assistance; and to take such other measures as may appear to them and you necessary for these great ends; promising to support them with the whole force of this Province; *always observing*, whatever plan of confederacy you enter into, *the regulating the internal police of this Province is to be reserved to the Colony Legislature.*"

The Convention of the Colony of Maryland, by a resolution (adopted June 28, 1776, and laid before Congress July 1), authorized and empowered the deputies of the Colony to —

"Concur with the other United Colonies, or a majority of them, in declaring the United Colonies free and independent, in favoring such further compact and confederation between them, in making foreign alliances, and in adopting such other measures as shall be judged necessary for securing the liberties of America; and that said Colony will hold itself bound by the resolutions of the majority of the United Colonies in the premises; *provided the sole and exclusive right of regulating the internal government and police of that Colony be reserved to the people thereof.*" — *Journals of Congress*, 1776, pp. 390, 391, 392.

The credentials of the Assembly of Rhode Island, after giving to the delegates power to enter into union and confederation, add, —

"Taking the greatest care to secure to this Colony, in the strongest and most perfect manner, its present established form, and all the powers of government, so far as relates to its internal police, and conduct of our affairs, civil and religious." — *Ibid.*, p. 343.

In the Revolutionary Government, in the Articles of Confederation, in the Constitution, in its judicial interpretation, in every administration under the Constitution, and in every department of the Government, the limitation has thus far been carefully recognized and faithfully kept. This familiar, well-settled doctrine, as to the independent respective spheres of the National and State Government, has never, perhaps, been more clearly and strongly stated than in one of the resolutions adopted by the Convention which ushered the present administration into power: —

"*Resolved*, That the maintenance inviolate of the rights of the States, and especially the right of each State to order and control its own domestic institutions according to its own judgment exclusively, is essential to that balance of powers on which the perfection and endurance of our political fabric depends."

It is expressed also, with clearness and strength, in the resolution adopted by the House, near the close of the last session of Congress, by a nearly unanimous vote: —

"*Resolved*, That neither the Federal Government, nor the people or governments of the non-slaveholding States, have a purpose or a constitutional right to legislate upon or interfere with slavery in any of the States of the Union."

These doctrines, as to the supremacy of the National Government within its sphere and of the reserved rights of the States, are elementary. Between them there is no necessary conflict. Each is the complement of the other, — both vital parts of that political system under whose admirable distribution and adjustment of powers the people of the United States have had for seventy years incomparably the best and most beneficent Government the world has ever known, — a Government now imperilled, not by reason of any inherent defect or any want of wisdom or foresight in its founders, not because we have outgrown its provisions, not because it is behind the age; but because it has fallen upon an age not worthy of it, — an age which has failed to appreciate the spirit of wisdom, prudence, and moderation, in which it was founded.

Such being the relation of the Government of the United States to its citizens and to the States, the first question that arises is, how far this relation is affected by the fact that several of the States have assumed, by ordinances of secession, to separate themselves from the Union.

The people of the United States, in and by the Constitution of the United States, established a National Government, without limitation of time, " for themselves and their posterity." It had been provided under the Articles of Confederation, that the Union should be perpetual. The Constitution was established to form "a more perfect union" than that of the Confederation; more efficient in power, and not less durable in time. There is not a clause or word in the Constitution, which looks to separation. It has careful provisions for its amendment, none for its destruction; capacity for expansion, none for contraction; a door for new States to come in, none for old or new ones to go out. An ordinance of secession has no legal meaning or force; is wholly inoperative and void. The Constitution, and the laws and treaties made under it, the people have declared, "shall be the supreme law of the land; and the judges in every State shall be bound thereby, any thing in the constitution or laws of any State to the contrary notwithstanding." The act of secession, therefore, cannot change in the least degree the legal relation of the State to the Union. No provision of the Constitution of the United States, no law or treaty of the United States, can be abrogated or impaired thereby. No citizen of the United States, residing in the seceded States, is, by such ordinance of secession, deprived of the just protection of, or exempted from any of his duties to, the United States. In contemplation of law, the reciprocal duties of protection and allegiance remain unaffected. After the act of secession, the province and duty of the Government of the United States are the same, according to the full measure of its ability, as before, — to enforce in every part of the Union, and over every inch of its territory, the Constitution and laws of the United States.

It is the necessary result of these principles, that no State can abrogate or forfeit the rights of its citizens to the protection of the Constitution of the United States, or the privileges and blessings of the Union which that Constitution secures and makes perpetual. The primary, paramount allegiance of every citizen of the United States is to the nation; and the State authorities can no more impair that allegiance than a county court or a village constable. Every proposition, however artfully disguised, which seeks to give any effect or vitality to an ordinance of secession, for evil or for good, is itself a confession of the right. To say that an act of secession is inoperative and void against the Constitution, and that this void act, sustained by force, is a practical abdication of the rights of the State under the Constitution, is to blow hot and blow cold, to deny and affirm, in the same breath; to state a proposition which is *felo de se.*

It is also the plain and necessary conclusion, from the principles before stated, that a *State* cannot commit treason. Under the Constitution of the United States, *persons* only can commit treason. How treason may be committed, and how tried and punished, the Constitution points out (Constitution, art. 3, sect. 3; Amendments, arts. 5 and 6). The persons who for the time being hold the offices under a State Government may individually commit treason; but the acts of the State officers, transcending their authority and in conflict with the Constitution of the United States, involve in their guilt no man who has not himself levied war against the United States, or adhered to their enemies, giving them aid and comfort. It is only we, the subjects, that can commit treason, or expiate its guilt. No man, or set of men, can, without our consent, involve us in the awful crime, or subject us to the awful penalties, of treason.

As a State cannot commit the crime of treason, it cannot incur a forfeiture of its powers and functions as the penalty of treason. The punishment provided for traitors is the result of judicial trial, conviction, and judgment. How to indict a State, the constitution of the court, the mode of trial, the form of judgment, and process of execution, yet exist *in gremio legis.* Nor is it material that the acts of the State officers have the sanction and support of the majority of the people of the State. Within the proper sphere of the State Government, the rule of the majority will prevail, except so far as it is restrained by the organic law; but the majority of the voters of the State cannot deprive the minority of the rights secured to them by the Constitution of the United States. Some of these rights may be kept in abeyance. Their exercise may be overborne by superior physical force. They may sleep; but it is not the sleep of death. They are integral parts of the Constitution, and can only perish when the Constitution perishes.

The State of Tennessee, for example, has passed an ordinance of "secession." She has allied herself with the other seceding States. Her vote of secession is sustained by force. Upon this new and startling theory of the Constitution, she has already incurred a forfeiture of all those functions and powers essential to the continued existence of the State as a body politic. The voice of her eloquent senator is heard in the Capitol; her venerable judge sits in the highest judicial tribunal, and exercises the highest functions of Government; her representatives mingle in our councils; her loyal citizens greet with tears of joy the banner of our advancing hosts, — their hope and our hope, their pride and our pride. Yet, upon this theory, there is no Tennessee: "the Commonwealth itself is past and gone." Its citizens can no longer be represented in this House or the Senate. The courts of the United States are closed against them (Corporation of New Orleans *vs.* Winter, 1 Wheaton Rep., 91). The requisition upon the State for troops was a mistake. The direct tax was a mistake. Its citizens, under the shield of the Constitution, are outlaws, and in their own homes exiles. If such be the effects of a void act of secession, we should be grateful we are not called upon to witness the results of a valid one. There is nothing in these doctrines of nullification or secession more disloyal to the Constitution, more fatal to the Union, than this doctrine of State suicide. It is the gospel of anarchy, the philosophy of dissolution. Nor by carrying out this doctrine of the destruction or forfeiture of the State organization would any thing be gained for the cause of freedom. Slavery exists by the local, municipal law; and would not be abolished, unless you go one step further, and hold, that, with the loss of the State organization, the institutions, laws, and civil relations of the States perish. Now, in case of conquest even, though the people of the conquered territory change their allegiance, their relations to each other and their rights of property remain undisturbed. The modern usage of nations, which has become law, would be violated if private property should be generally confiscated and private rights annulled (United States *vs.* Percheman, 7 Peters, 51; 3 Phillimore, p. 743). When, therefore, States were reduced to Territories, the National Government could not abolish slavery therein, except under the right of eminent domain and by giving just compensation.

If we are right as to the nullity of the acts of secession, we may proceed to inquire whether the fact, that the seceding States have attempted to form a new alliance or confederation, will effect the result. Upon the plainest letter of the Constitution, as well as by its entire spirit, these acts of confederation are void. Continuing as States in spite of their ordinances, they were expressly forbidden to enter into any treaty, alliance, or confederation, or into any agreement or compact, with another State or with a foreign power (Constitution, art. 1, sect. 10). Neither by secession nor confederation have they changed their legal relation to the Union and the Constitution of the United States. They are still members of the Union, foregoing for a time its privileges, but subject to its duties, bound to it by a cord which the sword of successful revolution can alone sever.

What, then, it may be asked, is the legal character of this great insurrection? The answer is, It is a rebellion of citizens of the United States against the Government of the United States; an organized effort to subvert and overthrow its authority, and to establish another Government in its stead. Nothing can be more explicit than the proclamation of April 15, 1861: —

"The laws of the United States have been for some time past and now are opposed, and the execution thereof obstructed, in the States of South Carolina, Georgia, Alabama, Florida, Mississippi, Louisiana, and Texas, by combinations too powerful to be suppressed by the ordinary course of judicial proceedings, or by the powers vested in the marshals by law.

"Now, therefore, I, Abraham Lincoln, President of the United States, in virtue of the power in me vested by the Constitution and the laws, have thought fit to call forth, and hereby do call forth, the militia of the several States of the Union, to the aggregate number of seventy-five thousand, *in order to suppress said combinations, and to cause the laws to be duly executed.*

"I appeal to all loyal citizens to favor, facilitate, and aid this effort to maintain the honor, the *integrity*, and the *existence of our National Union* and the perpetuity of popular Government, and to redress wrongs already long enough endured."

The State organizations have been found convenient, and have been used for the purposes of the Rebellion. Those of counties and cities have been used for the same ends. In either case, it was an entire perversion of their functions; and the action is none the less illegal and revolutionary on that account. A State, as such, having no power to engage in war with any other State or with the United States, cannot interpose its shield between the Government of the United States and its subjects committing treason by levying war against it; nor is such levying war any the less treason because the traitors held places of trust in the State Governments, and perverted the functions of those Governments to their base ends. Morally, it is an aggravation of the offence. It does not change its essential legal character.

In the Convention for forming the Constitution of the United States, Luther Martin, of Maryland, was anxious to insert a provision to save the citizens of the States from being punishable as traitors to the United States when acting expressly in obedience to the authority of their own States. The provision offered by him was, —

"That no act or acts done by one or more of the States against the United States, or by any citizen of any one of the United States, under the authority of one or more of the said States, shall be deemed *treason*, or *punished as such;* but, in case of war being levied by one or more of the States against the United States, the conduct of each party towards the other, and their adherents respectively, shall be regulated by the laws of war and of nations."

This proposition was rejected, Mr. Martin says with much feeling, because the leading members of the Convention meant to leave the States at the mercy of the National Government. The more obvious reason is, that it was inconsistent with the whole theory of the Constitution, which, springing from the people of the United States, acted directly upon them as its subjects, and with a force which no law or ordinance of a State could impair.

This, then, is not a conflict of States; nor is it a war of countries or of geographical lines. It is a conflict between Government and its disobedient subjects. He only is the enemy of the United States who is committing treason by levying war against the United States, or giving aid and comfort to those who do. The loyal, faithful subject of the United States, wherever on the soil of his country he may have his home, is not the enemy of his country. No subtilty of logic, no ingenuity of legal construction, no misapplication of the laws of international war to this contest, can change the nature of things; can convert loyalty into treason, or devotion into hostility. If there be to-day in Tennessee or Georgia, or South Carolina even, a loyal subject of the United States, " faithful among the faithless found," the Government is not at war with him. I am aware, that, as to property taken on the high seas, some of the district courts of the United States have held otherwise; but I venture to hope, that the court of last resort will affirm the doctrine, stated by Mr. Justice Nelson of that court, to be good sense and sound law: —

" On the breaking-out of a war between two nations, the citizens or subjects of the respective belligerents are deemed by the law of nations to be the enemies of each other. The same is true, in a qualified sense, in the case of a civil war arising out of an insurrection or rebellion against the mother-government. But, in the latter case, the citizens or subjects residing within the insurrectionary district, not implicated in the rebellion, but adhering to their allegiance, are not enemies, nor to be regarded as such. This distinction was constantly observed by the English Government in the disturbances in Scotland, under the Pretender and his son, in the years 1715 and 1745. It modifies the law as it respects the condition of the citizens or subjects, residing within the limits of the revolted district, who remain loyal to the Government."

The difference between a war and a rebellion is clear and vital. War is the hostile relation of one nation to another, involving all the subjects of both : rebellion is the relation which disloyal subjects hold to the nation, not involving or impairing the rights of loyal subjects. The law may fail to protect obedient subjects; but it never condemns them. As between the Government, and its subjects in arms against it, the *legal* relation is not that of war, notwithstanding the war-power is used to subdue and reduce them to obedience. Though the Rebellion has assumed gigantic proportions, and the civil power is impotent to repress it, the array of numbers, and extent of physical force, do not change its essential legal character. It is still treason, — the levying of war against the United States by those who owe to it allegiance. For this exigency the Constitution has provided. The war-power of the Government may be evoked " to execute the laws of the Union, and to suppress insurrection." In levying war against the United States, the rebels do not cease to be traitors, but are doing *the* thing in which the Constitution declares treason to consist (art. 3, sect. 3).

While using the powers and appliances of war for the purpose of subduing the Rebellion, we are by no means acting without the pale of the Constitution. We are using precisely the powers with which the Constitution has clothed us for this end. We are seeking domestic tranquillity by the sword the Constitution has placed in our hands. In the path of war, as of peace, the Constitution is our guide and our light, the cloud by day, the pillar of fire by night.

While using the powers of war for executing the laws and subduing rebellion, we are, of course, bound and restrained by the laws of war. It is our duty and our privilege to respect the maxims of humanity and moderation by which the law of nations and of Christian civilization has tempered the spirit of modern hostilities. During the war, we may recognize in the rebels the rights of belligerents; may send them flags of truce; may make with them capitulations, cartels for exchange of prisoners; and extend to them the courtesies which mitigate, to some extent, the iron rigor of war. These things were done in the earliest stages of our Revolution, not only before the separation of the Colonies was declared, but before the idea of independence had fairly taken possession of the public mind. But it was never supposed, that, by adopting the usages of civilized warfare, Great Britain was relaxing her hold upon the Colonies, or elevating them into independent powers. Nothing is, I think, plainer in principle, than that the recognition of these rights and the observance of these usages —*flagrante bello*— cannot affect the legal relation of the parties; does not divest the sovereign of his power, or release the subject from his duties, when the strife of arms ceases. It is only when rebellion has ripened into successful revolution, that the permanent legal relations of the parties are changed. The recognition of the " belligerent rights" of the rebels by foreign powers, can, as between the sovereign and his subjects, have no other or further effect. Such recognition (if known to the law of nations) proceeds upon the ground, that the *revolution is not accomplished, and that the connection is not dissolved*. Had this been done, the recognition would have been of their separate national existence.

In my humble judgment, Mr. Chairman, the " seceded States" (so called), and the people of those States, are to-day integral parts of the Union, over whom, when the conflict of arms ceases, the Constitution of the United States, and the laws made under it, will resume their peaceful sway. Traitors may perish; some institutions may perish: the nation will remain; and the States will remain, essential parts of the body politic. " The body is one, and hath many members; and all the members of that body, being many, are one body."

With this brief and imperfect development of the principles involved in this great controversy, I proceed to a more direct consideration of the subjects of confiscation and emancipation.

In seeking to know what this Government ought to do in relation to the confiscation of private property, or the emancipation of slaves, in the "seceding" States, the obvious question presenting itself to every mind at the threshold is, What is *the end* which the Government and the people are seeking to attain? There can be but one loyal answer to that question. It is to preserve the Union and the Constitution in their integrity; to vindicate in every part of this indivisible Republic its supreme law. No purpose, however humane, beneficent, or attractive, can divert our steps from the plain, straight path of sworn duty. What is writ is writ. In seeking to change it by force of arms, we become the rebels we are striving to subdue.

It is a plain proposition, that, in seeking to enforce the law, we are, as far as possible, to obey the law. We are not to destroy in seeking to preserve. The people do not desire a bitter and remorseless struggle over the dead body of the Constitution. We may raise armies and navies, and pour out as water the treasure and life-blood of the people; but we can neither think nor act wisely, live well, or die well, for the Republic, unless we keep clearly and always in view the end of all our labors and sacrifices, — the Union of our fathers, and the Constitution, which is its only bond. No thoughtful man can believe there is a possibility of reconstructing the Union on any other basis; or that it is within the province of Congress, in any other but the peaceful way of amendment, to make the effort.

The bills and joint resolutions before the House, propose, with some differences of policy and method, two measures, — the confiscation of the property of the rebels, and the emancipation of their slaves. Some of the resolutions propose the abolition of slavery itself,

CONFISCATION. 19

with compensation for loyal masters. It is my duty to examine, as briefly as I may, the wisdom, the justice, and the constitutionality of the measures proposed. And, first, of confiscation.

The propositions for confiscation include the entire property of the rebels, real and personal, for life and in fee. Within the class whose estates are to be confiscated are included not only those personally engaged in the Rebellion, in arms against the Government, but also those who adhere to them, giving them aid or comfort: so that within the sweep of the bills would be brought substantially the property of eleven States and six millions of people.

The mind instinctively shrinks from a proposition like this. It relucts to include in one "fell swoop" a whole people. It asks anxiously, if no consideration is to be had for different degrees of guilt; if the same measure is to be meted to those who organized the Rebellion and those who have been forced into it; if no consideration is to be given to the fact, that allegiance and protection are reciprocal duties; and that, for the last ten months, the National Government has found itself incapable of giving protection to its loyal subjects in the " seceding States,"— neither defending them, nor giving them arms to defend themselves; and that, deprived of our protection and incapable of resistance, they have yielded only to superior force; if a wise Government is to forget the nature of man and the influences of birth, of soil, of home, of society, and of State, by which his opinions are insensibly moulded; and that this pestilent heresy of the right of secession, fatal as it is now seen to be, not only to the existence of good government, but of social order itself, has been a cardinal article in the faith of a large portion of the people in the Southern States; and that they have been induced, by the arts and sophistries and falsehoods of unprincipled leaders, to believe that their future safety and well-being required the exercise of the right. Those leaders should atone for their crime by the just penalty of the law. But you cannot, says Burke, indict " a whole people;" you cannot apply to them the ordinary rules of criminal jurisprudence. To state the proposition to confiscate the property of eleven States is to confute it; is to shock our common sense, and sense of justice; is to forget not only the ties of history and of kindred, but those of a common humanity; is to excite the indignation of the civilized world, and to invoke the interposition of all Christian governments.

It is said that just retaliation requires the confiscation of the property of the rebels. Doubtless nations may feel compelled to resort to measures of severe retaliation; it may be their only security against future outrage: but a firmly established government does not resort to cruelty and injustice because its rebellious subjects have done so. It must maintain a higher standard of rectitude and justice. Its object is, not vengeance, but to deter men from crime. It knows that harsh and severe punishments but rouse pity for the criminal, and indignation against the Government.

Nor will the difference between confiscation by the rebels and by this Government be overlooked. Our acts of confiscation, if within the limits of the Constitution, are effective and permanent: theirs, void in law, are temporary in their effect. The title to one square inch of land will not be changed by any confiscation by the rebel authorities. Every man who has occupied the land of a loyal citizen under their pretended acts of confiscation will be liable for the full rent and damages to the estate. Every man who is in possession of personal property under them will be compelled to disgorge. Every debt paid under them into rebel treasuries will still be due to the loyal creditor. The restoration and indemnity will, I know, be imperfect. Many grievous wrongs will go unredressed; but every rebel, whatsoever functions he may have usurped, — judicial or executive, — who has invaded the rights of person or of property of a loyal citizen, will be liable to his last farthing for indemnity. So far, therefore, as our Government confiscates the property of rebels to its own use, it takes from the loyal citizen the sources to which he may justly look for redress.

The acts of general confiscation proposed would defeat the great end the Government has in view, — the restoration of order, union, and obedience to law. They would take from the rebels every motive for submission; they would create the strongest possible motives to continued resistance. In the maintenance of the Confederate Government, they might possibly find protection; in the restoration of ours, spoliation. *Spoliatis arma supersunt.* You leave them the great weapon of despair. Sallust said of the old Romans, " Majores nostri religiosissimi mortales nihil victis eripiebant præter injuriæ licentiam," — " Our ancestors, the most religious of men, took from the vanquished nothing but the license of wrong-doing," — " words," says Grotius, " worthy of having been said by a Christian."

It seems to be taken for granted, that our efforts to suppress the Rebellion will be successful in proportion to the *severity* of the measures we adopt. The assumption is at war with the lessons of history and with the nature of man. The most vigorous prosecution of the war possible is best for the Government and its subjects in arms against it. But the war is means to an end. "Wise men labor in the hope of rest, and make war for the sake of peace." It is only when justice is tempered with mercy that it is justice.

Apart from the injustice and impolicy of these acts of sweeping confiscation, I have not been able to find in the Constitution the requisite authority to pass them. There are two aspects in which the legal question may be viewed, — *first*, the confiscation and forfeiture of property as the punishment for crime; *secondly*, under what has popularly been called the "war-power" of the Government.

Looking at confiscation as the penalty of crime, treason, or any lower grade of offence, some things seem to be plain : —

That such forfeiture can be created by statutes applicable only to offences committed after their passage. Congress cannot pass an *ex post facto* law (Constitution, art. 1, sect. 9).

The subject charged with treason may justly claim all the muniments and safeguards of the Constitution.

He cannot be deprived of life, liberty, or property, without due process of law (Amendments, art. 5); that is, judicial process, as understood from the days of Magna Carta.

He cannot be held to answer for a capital or otherwise infamous crime, except in cases arising in the land or naval forces, or in the militia when in actual service in time of war or public danger, unless on presentment or indictment by a grand jury (*ibid.*).

After indictment, he must have a trial by an impartial jury of the State and district wherein the crime shall have been committed; which district shall have been previously ascertained by law (art. 3, sect. 2; Amendments, art. 6).

No attainder of treason can work a forfeiture, except during the life of the person attainted (Constitution, art. 3, sect. 2). By attainder is here clearly meant judicial attainder; as a bill of attainder (that is, an act of the Legislature) is, by a prior provision of the Constitution, expressly forbidden (art. 1, sect. 9).

These sacred provisions of the Constitution, which, as common-law muniments of life, liberty, and property, have existed in substance for six centuries, — " the least feeling their care, and the greatest not exempted from their power," — lie directly in the path, and are fatal obstructions to any legislation confiscating property as the penalty of treason, except as the result of the judicial trial and sentence of the offender.

It has been assumed, — I think, without sufficient reflection, — that, under our laws against treason, the most obnoxious traitors even will escape the righteous punishment of their crimes, because they must be tried by a jury in the State and district wherein the offence shall have been committed. Their only escape will be by exile. Where war is actually levied against the United States, where bodies of men have been actually assembled to effect by force of arms their treasonable purposes, all those who perform any part, however minute or however remote from the scene of action, and who are actually leagued in the general conspiracy, are to be considered as traitors (*Ex parte* Bolman, &c., 4 Cranch, 75). We have not, indeed, adopted the law of constructive presence, which holds that a man who incites or procures a treasonable act, is, by force of the incitement or procurement merely, legally present at the act. But it may be sufficient to constitute presence, if he is in a situation in which he can co-operate with any act of hostility, or furnish counsel and assistance to the parties if attacked (United States *vs.* Burr, 4 Cranch, 470). The modern facilities of communication greatly enlarge the field of co-operation. A commander at the end of a telegraph-wire, directing the assault upon a fort of the United States, or at a railroad station with troops ready to be moved to the assistance of the rebel army in action, is, in law, present at the overt acts of treason. The leaders of this Rebellion will be found, therefore, to have committed treason, and to be liable to indictment and trial in many States and districts in which a jury will be ready, upon adequate proof, to convict.

In the proposed measures, the thing sought to be done is the confiscation of the property of the rebel as the penalty of his offence, and the attainment of this end without the trial and conviction of the offender. Though, under the Constitution, upon a trial and *conviction* of a traitor, you can only take the life estate, these measures assume, that, without any trial or conviction, you may take the fee-simple. Our legal instincts shrink from such a proposition. Its intrinsic difficulties have been seen and felt; and a resort has been had to analogies and precedents, judicial and legislative, to find for it some sanction and support; I think, without success.

1. It is true, as has been said, that, under the Constitution, men may be deprived of life and property without trial by jury. Cases arising in the land and naval forces, and in the militia when in actual service in time of war or public danger, are in terms excepted from the general rule (Amendments, art. 5); but the exception, instead of impairing, by the law of logic as of common sense, confirms the rule.

2. Property is taken for taxes, and certainly without trial by jury, where the tax, and mode of assessment, are valid; but this is under an express grant of power to Congress " to lay and collect taxes " (art. 1, sect. 8), the principle and general method of which were perfectly well understood when the Constitution was adopted. Nor does the exercise of this power, as has been suggested, take private property for public use without just compensation: on the contrary, the true and just theory of taxation is, that the price paid is the reasonable compensation for the protection and security of life, liberty, and property, which a wise and efficient government affords.

3. The forfeiture of goods for breach of the revenue-laws has slight, if any, analogy to the confiscation of property as a punishment for the crime of its owner. To Congress is given the power to "regulate commerce," and "to levy and collect imports;" and, of course, to prescribe the terms and conditions upon which goods may be imported. It may well avail itself of a familiar principle by which property used in violating, defeating, or defrauding the law is liable to forfeiture. Though the forfeiture of the common law did not, strictly speaking, attach *in rem*, but was a part or consequence of the judgment of conviction of the offender, this doctrine was never applied to seizures and forfeitures created by statute *in rem*, and cognizable on the revenue side of the exchequer. The thing was then primarily considered as the offender, and the offence was attached to *it*. The same principle is applied to proceedings *in rem*, and seizures in the admiralty (2 Wheaton, The Palmyra). It is upon this distinction that the statutes of July 19 and of Aug. 6, 1861, find their support. The principle is, that the thing used in violating the law may be seized and condemned without a judgment upon the guilt of the owner.

I proceed to inquire how far, if at all, the powers of Congress are enlarged by the existence of this Rebellion, and the use of the appliances of war to subdue it.

It would seem to be plain, that the resistance of any portion of the people to the Constitution and laws cannot operate to confer upon Congress any new substantive power, or to abrogate any limitations of the powers of Congress which the people have imposed. When the Constitution intends that the existence of war or rebellion shall put an end to any restriction on the power of the Government, it says so: when it does not say so, the fair inference is that it does not mean so. Examples of such removals of restraint are found in article one, section eight, providing that the privilege of the " writ of *habeas corpus* shall not be suspended, unless when, in cases of rebellion or invasion, the public safety may require it;" and in article three of the Amendments, forbidding, in time of peace, the quartering of soldiers in any house without the consent of the owner, but in time of war permitting it to be done " in a manner to be prescribed by law."

Engaged in suppressing a great and formidable rebellion, the Government may use the instrumentalities of war, so far as they are adapted to the end: but it is never freed from the restraints of the Constitution; can never rise above it. The Constitution is never silent in the midst of arms. In war, as in peace, it is the supreme law; itself *salus populi et suprema lex*.

When Government is compelled to use the power of war, it observes its limitations. How far, in the use of this power, it may confiscate, or subject to forfeiture, private property, is the next question before us.

Some things are tolerably well settled. That property used in promoting the rebellion, in levying war against the United States, is lawful prize of war. This would include the arms, munitions, and provisions of war, in actual use or procured for the purpose. The rule extends to goods used, not strictly as munitions or implements of war, but so as to defeat the military and naval operations resorted to to subdue the rebellion: as goods on their way to relieve besieged towns or forts; or ships or cargo violating a blockade, or proceeding to or from ports with which commercial intercourse has been interdicted. It may extend to ships and cargo upon the high seas, the property of those levying war against the United States; enemies, not because of their domicile or residence upon one part rather than another of the territory of the Union, but because they are in arms against it.

Perhaps we should add to these, requisitions or contributions, within military districts, levied upon those at war with the Government, for the support of the invading army. Such requisitions were, however, regarded by Wellington, a great statesman as well as great commander, as iniquitous; as a system for which the British soldier was unfit. I would refer also to the excellent remarks on this subject by President Woolsey, in his admirable Introduction to "International Law," p. 304.

Beyond the points suggested, it is believed the usages of international war do not extend. By the modern usages of nations, private property on the land is exempt from confiscation. This exemption, Mr. Wheaton says (and there is no higher authority), is now held to extend " to cases of the absolute and unqualified conquest of the enemy's country" (Wheaton's " Elements of International Law," p. 421). We refer also, as tending to the same result, to Vattel, book 3, chap. 8, sect. 147; to 1 Kent's "Commentaries," pp. 102, 104; 3 Phillimore, p. 140; Woolsey, p. 304. To this mitigated rule of war, there are doubtless exceptions. Of these, Mr. Wheaton says, —

"The exceptions to these general mitigations of the extreme rights of war, considered as a contest of force, all grow out of the same original principle of natural law, which authorizes us to use against an enemy such a degree of violence, and such only, as may be necessary to secure the object of hostilities. The same general rule which determines how far it is lawful to destroy the persons of enemies, will serve as a guide in judging how far it is lawful to ravage or lay waste their country. If this be necessary in order to accomplish the just ends of war, it may be lawfully done; but not otherwise. Thus, if the progress of an enemy cannot be stopped, nor our own frontier secured, or if the approaches to a town intended to be attacked cannot be made, without laying waste the intermediate territory, the extreme case may justify a resort to measures not warranted by the ordinary purposes of war." — Page 421.

The exceptions growing out of military exigencies, and measured and governed by them, cannot be foreseen and provided for by legislation, but must be left, where the law of nations leaves them, with the military commander.

It has been said that these acts of general confiscation find support under the provision of the Constitution which authorizes Congress " to make rules concerning captures by land and water." The Constitution does not define the meaning of the word " captures." It refers us in such cases to the law of nations, as in others to the common law. Congress has power to declare " war." What war is, the just causes of war, the rights and duties of nations in conducting it, are to be found in the law of nations. The " captures " referred to are very plainly not seizures of property under legal process, confiscation, or forfeiture, but the taking of enemy's property by force or strategy, *jure victoriæ*. The title is acquired by capture, and liable to be lost by recapture. To make rules concerning "captures" is not to make rules in conflict with or beyond the law of nations. The extent to which the power conferred by the law of nations shall be exercised, and the disposition to be had of captures when made, are the proper subjects of municipal law, and of the provision of the Constitution.

The case of Brown *vs.* the United States (8 Cranch, 110) has been cited as expressly deciding that Congress has power to pass a confiscation bill. I submit, with great respect, that it decides no such thing. The only point *decided* in the case was, that British property found in the United States, on land, at the commencement of international hostilities (war of 1812), could not be condemned as enemy's property, without an act of Congress for that purpose. The court, dealing with a question arising under war with a foreign nation, had no occasion to consider the powers or duties of Congress in the case of rebellion. The *discussions* of the court recognize a distinction between the right of the sovereign to take the persons and confiscate the property of the enemy wherever found, and the mitigations of the rule which the humane usages of modern times have introduced. With all my reverence for the great magistrate who delivered the opinion of the court, I must be permitted to say, that usage is itself the principal source of the law of nations, and that these humane usages have become the rules of war in Christian States. The law of nations, says Bynkershoek, is only a presumption founded on usage (*De foro Legatorum*, chap. 18, sect. 6).

It is suggested, that, if the confiscation of private property violated the law of nations, the courts could not overrule the interpretation of that law by the political department of the Government, and that no other power could intervene. Possibly this may be so; but surely it is not intended that we shall violate the law of nations in dealing with our subjects, because there is no appeal or redress for the subject. It is in the exercise of irresponsible power that the nicest sense of justice, and the greatest caution and forbearance, are demanded. In suppressing a rebellion so atrocious, marked by such fury and hate against a Government felt only in its blessings, forbearance seems to us weakness, and vengeance the noblest of virtues; but, in our calmer moments, we hear the Divine Voice: "Vengeance is mine; I will repay."

I conclude what I have to say upon this branch of the subject with the remark, that, in substance and effect, the bills before the House seek the permanent forfeiture and confiscation of property, real and personal, without the trial of the offender. I am unable to see how, under the Constitution, that result can be reached.

The temporary use of property in districts under military occupation, and of estates abandoned by their owners, rests upon distinct principles, which it is not now necessary to consider. We have only to remark, in passing, that the use of such property and the rule in such districts can be provisional only, waiting the regular action of the State governments, and in no way impairing their permanent powers.

I proceed to the question of the deepest interest involved in this discussion, — the emancipation of slaves in the "seceding States." There is no subject on which our feelings are so likely to warp our judgment; in which calmness is so necessary and so difficult, and declamation so easy or so useless. The general principles stated in relation to the power and duty of Congress as to confiscation are applicable to the subject of emancipation.

On the question of policy, the plausible and attractive argument is, that the only effectual way to suppress rebellion is to remove its cause. The position, when thoroughly probed, is, not that the National Government has not the power to put down the rebellion without resort to emancipation, but that the continued existence of slavery is incompatible with the future safety of the Republic. This plainly is not a question of present military necessity, but one affecting the permanent structure of the Government, and involving material changes in the Constitution. This can be done in one of two ways: in the method the Constitution points out; or by successful revolution on the part of the free States, and the entire subjugation of the slave States. No man can foresee to-day what policy a severe and protracted struggle *may* render necessary. It is sufficient to say, that into such a war of conquest and extermination the people of the United States have no *present* disposition to enter. They have too thorough a conviction of the capacity of the Government to subdue the Rebellion by the means the Constitution sanctions, to be desirous of looking beyond its pale.

Upon the legal aspect of the question, it may be

stated, as a general proposition, that Congress, in time of peace, has no power over slavery in the States. By that is meant the institution itself; for the National Government may, in my judgment, forfeit the right of the master in the labor of the slave, as a penalty for crime of which the master shall be convicted; and, when so forfeited, it may dispose of the right as it sees fit. Nor is there any intrinsic difficulty in the use of this species of property under the right of eminent domain. If the Government were constructing a fort or digging an intrenchment, it might hire this species of labor, or, if necessary, take it, as it might other labor or property, giving reasonable compensation therefor.

The provision as to the return of fugitives from service cannot be deemed an exception to the general rule before stated; for the provision applies to escapes from one State into another, and not to escapes within the State. Of which we may remark, in passing, that, as to the former class, the power of the Government is strictly civil, to be executed by judicial process; and that, as to the latter, the National Government, in time of war or peace, has no concern.

Nor would an act of the National Government liberating the slaves within a State, having the consent of the State and providing compensation for the masters, militate with the rule. *Conventio vincet legem.* The consent of the State would relieve the difficulty.

But the question arises, how far the existence of the Rebellion confers upon Congress any new power over the relation of master and slave. Strictly speaking, no new power is conferred upon any department of the

Government by war or rebellion; but it may have powers to be used in those exigencies which are dormant in time of peace. Such, for example, are the power to call out the militia (art. 1, sect. 8), to try by martial law cases arising in the militia (Amendments, 5), to suspend the writ of *habeas corpus* (art. 1, sect. 9), to quarter troops in private houses (Amendments, 3). But, when the National Government is called to the stern duty of repressing insurrection or repelling invasion, may not new power over the relation of master and slave be brought into action? Such, I think, is the result.

A plain case is presented by slaves employed in the military and naval service of the rebels. If captured, they may be set free.

The Government may refuse to return a slave to a master who has been engaged in the Rebellion, or suffered the slave to be employed in it.

It may require the services of all persons subject to its jurisdiction by residing upon its territory, when the exigency arises, to aid in executing the laws, in repressing insurrection, or repelling invasion. This right is, in my judgment, paramount to any claim of the master to his labor, under the local law. There might be a question of the duty of the slave to obey; but the will of the master could not intervene. His claim, if any, would be a reasonable compensation for the labor of his slave.

But, though the power may exist, there is, with prudent and humane men, no desire to use it. Nothing but the direst extremity would excuse the use of a power fraught with so great perils to both races; and the recent triumphs of our arms, evincing our capacity to subdue the Rebellion without departure from the usages of civilized warfare, have, I trust, indefinitely postponed the question.

There is one other exigency in which the relation of master and slave must give way to military necessity. If the commander of a military district shall find that the slaves within it, by the strength they give to their rebellious masters, — by bearing arms, or doing other military service, or acting as the servants of those who do, — obstruct his efforts to subdue the Rebellion, he may deprive the enemy of this force, and may remove the obstruction, by giving freedom to the slaves. This, it is apparent, is not a civil or legislative, but a strictly military right and power, springing from the exigency, and measured and limited by it, to be used for the subduing of the enemy, and for no ulterior purpose. If the commander-in-chief and the generals under him shall observe faithfully this distinction, the use of the power ought to be no just ground of complaint. If, in consequence of the protraction of the war, the effect of the use of this power should be to put an end to slavery in any of the States, or to weaken and impair its force, we may justly thank God for bringing good out of evil.

In my judgment, it would be impracticable for the Legislature, even if it had the power, to anticipate by any general statute the exigencies or prescribe the rules for the exercise of this power. The Legislature and the people will be content to leave the matter to the sound discretion and patriotism of the magistrate selected to execute the laws.

To avoid misconstruction, I desire to say that the

power of Congress over slavery in this District is absolute; that no limitation exists in the letter or spirit of the Constitution or the acts of cession. All that is requisite for abolishing slavery here is *just* compensation to the master. Equally absolute, in my judgment, is the power of Congress over slavery in the Territories.

Mr. Chairman, in a letter to a friend, published on the first day of the last year, I ventured to say that secession should be resisted to the last extremity, by force of arms; that it cost us seven years of war to secure this Government, and that seven years, if need be, would be wisely spent in the struggle to maintain it; that for this country there was no reasonable hope of peace but within the pale of the Constitution, and in obedience to its mandates. The progress of events has served only to deepen those convictions. They are as firmly rooted as my trust in God and his providence. Whoever else may falter, I must stand by the Constitution I have sworn to support. I am not wise enough to build a better. I am not rash enough to experiment upon a nation's life. There is, to me, no hope of "one country" but in this system of many States and one nation, working in their respective spheres as if the Divine Hand had moulded and set them in motion. To this system the integrity of the States is as essential as that of the central power. Their life is one life. A consolidated government for this vast country would be essentially a despotic government, democratic in name, but kept buoyant by corruption, and efficient by the sword.

Desiring the extinction of slavery with my whole mind and heart, I watch the working of events with devout gratitude and with patience. The last year has done the work of a generation. By no rash act of ours, much less any radical change in the Constitution, shall we hasten the desired result. If, in the pursuit of objects however humane; if, beguiled by the flatteries of hope or of shallow self-conceit; if, impelled by our hatred of treason, and desire of vengeance or retribution; if, seduced by the "insidious wiles of foreign influence," we yield to such change, we shall destroy the best hope of freeman and slave, and the best hope of humanity this side the grave.

CONFISCATION.

May 24, 1862.

The House having under consideration the bills to confiscate the property, and free from servitude the slaves, of rebels, Mr. THOMAS said,—

Mr. SPEAKER,— Before proceeding to the discussion of the measures before the House, I hope I may be pardoned for making one or two preliminary suggestions. At an early day, I expressed my earnest conviction of the course to be pursued by the Government and people of this country in relation to secession; that it was but another and an unmanly form of rebellion, and that it must be met at the threshold, and crushed by arms; that after an ordinance of secession, as before, it was the duty of the Government to execute in every part of this indivisible Republic the Constitution and the laws.

But I believed then, and believe now, that the life of the States is just as essential a part of this Union as the life of the central power; that their life is indeed one life; and when the gentleman from New York [Mr. Sedgwick] yesterday assured the House that the statement made by me in a former speech, "that, when the conflict of arms ceases, the nation will remain, and the

States will remain essential parts of the body politic," "was one of those bold and audacious propositions which cannot fail to shock the common sense of mankind," I felt that either he or I had wholly misconceived the nature and structure of the Government under which we live. *E pluribus unum;* Of many States, one nation. The Union is not a graveyard for the burial of dead commonwealths. The body politic is safer with a severed limb than with a dead one. But the gentleman from New York has made progress in this doctrine of State suicide, and assures the House not only of the death of the States, but that the people, " by permission of the military power, and not before," can form new governments, and seek again admission here. Mark the words, " by permission of the military power, and not before." Where are we drifting, Mr. Speaker? and what is the end? These are not hasty words, but the deliberately uttered language of one, who, no less by culture and capacity than by your appointment, is a leader of the House. " By permission of the military power, and not before." I repeat the question, Where are we drifting? What is the end?

I was guilty of another audacious act in the view of the gentleman from New York. I awoke " St. Paul from the dead " to give countenance to my doctrine. The gentleman must pardon me, Mr. Speaker. I must be an old fogy. It never occurred to me that the Epistles of Paul were among the dead things of the past. I supposed they were the well-springs of immortal life, and, like the Gospels, the same to-day, yesterday, and for ever. I am bound to presume this was a heedless remark; for I am sure the gentleman can have no sympathy with the new school of philosophy which has outgrown the gospel, and which, making equal war with the Christian Church and with the Union, has issued the new evangel, in which abstract love of the race is substituted for practical love of our neighbor, confusion for social order, freedom from restraint for the liberty of obedience. But let this pass.

Mr. Speaker, no man can desire more earnestly than I do the suppression of this Rebellion, and the restoration of order, unity, and peace. But there are two things I cannot, I will not do. I will not trample beneath my feet the Constitution I have sworn before God to support. I will not violate, even against these rebels, the law of nations as recognized and upheld by all civilized and Christian States. I believe I must do both to vote for these bills, and at the same time do an act unwise, and especially adapted to defeat the end in view, if that end be the restoration of the Union and the salvation of the Republic.

I propose, very briefly, to examine the bills before the House (and especially that as to the confiscation of property), under the law of nations and under the Constitution of the United States, and then to say a word upon their policy.

The positions assumed by the friends of these measures are, that we may deal with those engaged in this Rebellion as public enemies and as traitors; that, regarding them as enemies, we may use against them all the powers granted by the law of nations, and, viewing them as rebels or traitors, we may use against them all the powers granted by the Constitution; and that, in either view, these bills can be sustained.

Dealing with them as public enemies, it is said, that, under the existing law of nations, we have a clear right to confiscate the entire private property, on the land as well as the sea, real and personal, of those in arms, and of non-combatants who may in any way give aid and comfort to the Rebellion. This first bill sweeps over the whole ground. I deny the proposition, Mr. Speaker. In the name of that public law whose every humane sentiment it violates; in the name of that civilization whose amenities it forgets and whose progress it overlooks; in the name of human nature itself, whose better instincts it outrages, I deny it. Such is not the law of nations.

To give a plausible aspect to the proposition, the advocates of this bill have gone back to Grotius and to Bynkershoek for the rules of war; and even then have omitted to give what Grotius calls the *temperamenta*, or restraints upon the rules. You might as well attempt to substitute the code of Moses for the beatitudes of the gospel. Any thing can be established by such resort to the authorities. By the older writers, you can prove not only all the property of the vanquished may be taken, but that every prisoner may be put to death. By Grotius, I can show that all persons taken in war are slaves, and that this is the lot even of all found within the enemy's boundaries when the war broke out; that this iron rule applies, not to men only, but to their wives and children; nay, further, that the master has over the slaves the power of life and death. — *De Jure*

Belli et Pacis, book 3, chap. 7, sects. 1, 2, and 3. I cite a short passage from the chapter referred to: —

"The effects of this right are unlimited; so that the master may do any thing lawfully to the slave, as Seneca says. There is no suffering which may not be inflicted on such slaves with impunity; no act which may not in any manner be commanded or extorted: so that even cruelty in the masters towards persons of servile condition is unpunished, except so far as the civil law imposes limits, and punishments for cruelty. In all nations alike, says Caius, we may see that the masters have the power of life and death over slaves. He adds afterwards, that, by the Roman law, limits were set to this power; that is, on Roman ground. So Donatus in Terence: 'What is not lawful from a master to a slave?'"

By Bynkershoek, you may establish that the conqueror has over the vanquished the power of life and death, and the power of selling them into slavery; that every thing is lawful in war, — the use of poison and the destruction of the unarmed and defenceless. — *Law of War*, Duponceau's translation, pp. 2, 18, 19, 20.

But what then, Mr. Speaker? Does any man suppose that these writers give us the laws of war, as upheld, sanctioned, and used by the Christian and civilized States of to-day? Nothing would be further from the fact. Commerce, civilization, Christian culture, have tempered and softened the rigor of the ancient rules; and the State which should to-day assume to put them in practice would be an outcast from the society of nations. Nay, more: they would combine, and rightfully combine, to stay its hand. For the modern law of war, you must look to the usages of civilized States, and to the publicists who have explained and enforced them. Those usages constitute themselves the laws of war.

In relation to the capture and confiscation of private property on the land, I venture to say with great confidence, and after careful examination, that the result of the whole matter has never been better stated than by our own great publicist, Mr. Wheaton: —

"But by the modern usage of nations, which has now acquired the force of law, temples of religion, public edifices devoted to civil purposes only, monuments of art, and repositories of science, are exempted from the general operations of war. Private property on land is also exempt from confiscation, with the exception of such as may become booty in special cases, when taken from enemies in the field or in besieged towns, and of military contributions levied upon the inhabitants of the hostile territory. This exemption extends even to the case of an absolute and unqualified conquest of the enemy's country." — *Elements of International Law*, p. 421.

It is not too much to say, that no careful student of international law will deny that this passage from Mr. Wheaton fairly expresses the modern usage and law upon the subject; but you will permit me to refer for a moment to the doctrine stated by my illustrious predecessor, whose name has been so often invoked in this debate, John Quincy Adams. "Our object," he says in a letter to the Secretary of State, "is the restoration of all the property, including slaves, which, by the usages of war among civilized nations, ought not to have been taken." "All private property on shore was of that description. It was entitled by the laws of war to exemption from capture." — *Mr. Adams to the Secretary of State*, Aug. 22, 1815.

Again, he says, in a letter to Lord Castlereagh, Feb. 17, 1816, —

"But as, by the same usages of civilized nations, private property is not the subject of lawful capture in war upon the land, it is perfectly clear, that, in every stipulation, private property shall be respected; or that, upon the restoration of places during the war, it shall not be carried away." — 4 *American State Papers*, pp. 116, 117, 122, 123.

A volume might be filled with like citations from modern writers. I will content myself with perhaps the latest expression, and from a great statesman, a native of Massachusetts, and of my own county of Worcester: —

"The prevalence of Christianity and the progress of civilization have greatly mitigated the severity of the ancient mode of prosecuting hostilities. . . . It is a generally received rule of modern warfare, — so far, at least, as operations upon land are concerned, — that the persons and effects of non-combatants are to be respected. The wanton pillage or uncompensated appropriation of individual property by an army, even in possession of an enemy's country, is against the usage of modern times. Such a proceeding at this day would be condemned by the enlightened judgment of the world, unless warranted by particular circumstances. Every consideration which upholds this conduct in regard to a war on land favors the application of the same rule to the persons and property of citizens of the belligerents found upon the ocean." — *Mr. Marcy to the Count de Sartiges*, July 28, 1856.

Such I believe to be the settled law and usage of nations. A careful examination of the arguments made on this subject has served but to strengthen and deepen this conviction.

I do not forget, Mr. Speaker, that the case of Brown *vs.* The United States (8 Cranch, 110) has been often referred to in this debate as affirming the contrary rule. The points decided in that case I have before stated to the House. The points, the only points, decided were, that British property found in the United States on land at the commencement of hostilities (war of 1812) could

CONFISCATION. 45

not be condemned as enemy's property, without an act of Congress for that purpose ; and that the declaration of war was not sufficient. Gentlemen have referred to the *obiter dicta*, the discussions of the judges, as the decision of the court. The distinction is familiar and vital, but has been lost sight of in this debate. Only the points necessarily involved in the result constitute the decision. Let me illustrate the matter by a familiar case, — that of Dred Scott. It is the matter outside of the decision, what a distinguished jurist has called the "slopping-over" of the court, that was so fruitful in mischief. The point decided by the majority of the court was, that Dred Scott was not a citizen of Missouri, so as to be able to maintain an action in the courts of the United States, upon the grounds of such citizenship. Under the conflicting decisions in the courts of Missouri, I have always thought that case might have been decided either way, without attracting public attention or animadversion. All that was said outside of that point has no more legal force than the paper on which it was written. Use the sayings of the judges in that case, as they have used those in Brown *vs.* The United States, and you can establish the rightful existence of slavery in the Territories, the invalidity of the Missouri Compromise, and God only knows how many other errors in history and law. Treat what is said by the majority of the court outside of the point decided as argument,— and it is nothing more,— and slavery in the Territories is without any legal prop or support. And I may say, in passing, Mr. Speaker, there never was, in my judgment, a plausible argument even to establish the power and right of the master to take his slave into the Territories, and hold him in servitude. Slavery exists by local law and usage only. It has no extra territorial power. The moment the slave, with the consent of the master, is taken beyond the line of the place where the law tolerates its existence, the chains fall from his limbs. Property in the slave there may be by local municipal law, but not by the law of nature and of nations; not by that universal, immutable law of which Cicero speaks so divinely in the " Republic." May I give the Latin, Mr. Speaker? *Nec erit alia lex Romœ, alia Athenis, alia nunc, alia posthac; sed et omnes gentes et omni tempore una lex et sempiterna et immutabilis continebit.* Nobler thought in nobler words never fell from human lips or pen.

But I return from this digression to say, Mr. Speaker, that the distinction sought to be established by the passages cited from the discussions in the case of Brown *vs.* The United States, between the law of war and the mitigations of that law which the usages of modern nations have introduced, has no foundation in principle. It is in the usages of civilized and Christian nations that we are to seek the law of nations. As the law merchant has grown up from the usages of trade and commerce, so has the modern law of nations grown up from the usages of enlightened States. The ancient barbarous rules of war have been tempered and softened by commerce, by the arts, by diffused culture, and, more than all, by the spirit of the gospel; and all Christian States recognize with joy and with obedience the milder law. In the jurisprudence of nations, as in our own, there is one law felt above all others, — the law of progress. Apparently at rest, it is ever silently moving onward, quickened, purified, and illumined by the inspiration of that higher law, " whose seat is the bosom of God, and its voice the harmony of the world." The great, prophetic thought of Pascal may yet be realized: *Deux lois suffisent pour regler la république chrétienne, mieux que toutes les lois politiques, — l'amour de Dieu, et celui du prochain.*

I do not know that I can more fitly conclude what I can say, in the brief time allotted to me, on the capture and confiscation of the private property of rebels, viewed in the light of international law, than in the words of John Marshall, near the close of his judicial life : —

" It may not be unworthy of remark, that it is very unusual, even in cases of conquest, for the conqueror to do more than to displace the sovereign, and assume dominion over the country. The modern usage of nations, which has become law," —

mark the words, Mr. Speaker, — " the modern usage of nations, which has become law,"—

— " would be violated ; that sense of justice and of right, which is acknowledged and felt by the whole civilized world, would be outraged, — if private property should be generally confiscated, and private rights annulled. The people change their allegiance ; their relation to their ancient sovereign is dissolved : but their relations to each other, and their rights of property, remain undisturbed. If this be the modern rule, even in cases of conquest, who can doubt its application to the case of an amicable cession of territory ? " — *United States* vs. *Percheman*, 7 Peters, 51.

It is against the light of these considerations and authorities, and against the prevailing law and judgment of the Christian world, that it has been so often confidently, I will not say flippantly, asserted on this floor, that there could be no doubt of our power, under the law of nations, to seize and confiscate the entire property of the rebels as public enemies.

I pass to the second branch of the subject, our power, under the Constitution, to pass these bills. It has been often said in the course of this debate, and in terms without qualification, that the rebels hold to us the twofold relation of enemies and traitors, and that we may use against them all the appliances of war and all the penalties of municipal law. To a certain limited extent, the proposition is sound. Treason consists in levying war against the United States. The act of treason is an act of war, and you use the powers of war to meet and subdue traitors in arms against the Government.

It is also true, that, in the relations between the Government and its subjects, the rightful power of punishment does not necessarily cease with the war; but is it also true, that you can exercise both powers at the same time? And is not here the utter fallacy of this whole argument? Take an example. You have been accustomed to exchange flags of truce; you have recognized, to a certain extent, belligerent powers. An officer of the rebel army comes to you under a flag of truce: can you take him from under that flag, and hang him for treason? He stands to you in the double relation of enemy and traitor; but you cannot touch a hair of his head while he is under that white flag. Take another case. You have stipulated for an exchange of prisoners of war. The cartel has been sent, and the prisoner of war is on his way to make the exchange. Does any man on this floor say that you can take him on his way, and try and hang him? And if not, why not? The plain answer is, Because, having recognized him as under the law of nations, while he is subject to its power, he is entitled to its protection.

Pass what bills we may, Mr. Speaker, when the war is ended, these questions will come up to be settled. I hope I may be pardoned for saying, with great respect, to my friends on all sides of the House, that they will be as difficult questions as statesmen or jurists were ever called upon to decide; and that it is wise to reserve, as far as possible, our judgment. No thoughtful man will content himself with the declaration, that belligerent " rebels have no rights." Passion may say that; reason, never. Passion, sooner or later, subsides, and reason re-ascends the judgment-seat; and these questions must be answered there, and to that august tribunal before which the conduct of men and nations passes in view, — the enlightened opinion of the Christian world. Such questions are, how far, *flagrante bello* (while war was raging), with respect to prisoners of war, the civil power was restrained; how far the treating with rebels, and exchanging them as prisoners of war, may affect their punishment as traitors, either in person or property. I express no opinion, except to say they must be calmly met and answered.

But assuming, for the sake of the argument, that during the war even, and while recognizing their belligerent rights, you may visit upon the rebels the full force and weight of the municipal law, I proceed to inquire whether the mode proposed by these bills is in conformity to the organic and supreme law, the Constitution of the United States. I am not to be deterred from the discussion by any suggestions from weak or wicked men — none other can make them — of leniency to rebels, and compassion for traitors. There is but little elevation in contempt; but such suggestions do not rise high enough to meet it. They pass by me as the idle wind. If a man has no other arrows in his quiver, let him use these: I am content.

The favorite argument, Mr. Speaker, of those who claim for Congress the power to confiscate the property of traitors without trial by jury is, that the want of this power would show a fatal weakness in the Constitution, and a lack of wisdom and foresight in its framers. They will not believe the Constitution is so weak and helpless, so incapable of self-defence. Nothing, in my judgment, so shows its majesty and strength; pray God, immortal strength. The powers of war are almost infinite. The resources of this vast country spring to your open hand. All that men have, even their lives, are at the service of their country; and in this great conflict how nobly and freely given! You can raise an army of seven hundred thousand men; you can give them all the best appliances of war; you can cover your bays and rivers and seas with your navy; you can blockade a coast of three thousand miles; you may cut down the last rebel on the field of battle. Such is the power of war. But, Mr. Speaker, when you shall have used all these powers, when peace shall have been restored, or when the rebels shall come and lay themselves at your feet or be taken captive by your arms, then also will the power of that Constitution be made manifest; then also will this Government be shown to be the most powerful and the noblest on the earth, not because the captured rebel is at your mercy, but because he is not; because, under the shield of the Constitution, the rebel at your feet is stronger than armies, stronger than navies. You cannot touch a hair of his head, or take from him a dollar of his property, until you shall have tried and condemned him by the judgment of his peers and by the law of the land. Does this show the weakness of the Constitution, or does it show its transcendent strength? Are these written constitutions established to give to Government power without limit over the property, liberty, and life of the citizen? or are they made to define and limit the power of the Government, and to shield and protect the rights of the subject?

I have always been taught that the people is the sovereign; that these constitutions are carefully defined grants from the sovereign power, so framed as to establish justice, and at the same time secure the blessings of liberty and the protection of law even to the humblest and meanest citizen. I know, Mr. Speaker, that these are getting to be old-fashioned sentiments. Magna Carta is soiled and worm-eaten. The Bill of Rights, the muniments of personal freedom, habeas corpus, trial by jury, — what are they all worth in comparison with this new safeguard of liberty, "the proceeding *in rem*"?

Were you ever at Runnymede, Mr. Speaker? I

remember going down, on a beautiful day in July, from Windsor Castle to the plain, and crossing the narrow channel of the Thames to that little island, on which, more than six centuries ago, in the early gray of morning, those sturdy barons wrested from an unwilling king the first great charter of English freedom, the germ of life of the civil liberty we have to-day. I could hardly have been more moved, had I stood in the village and by the manger in which was cradled " the son of Mary and the Son of God." From the gray of that morning streamed the rays, which, uplifting with the hours, coursing with the years, and keeping peace with the centuries, have encircled the whole earth with the glorious light of English liberty, the liberty for which our fathers planted these commonwealths in the wilderness; for which they went through the baptism of fire and blood in the Revolution; which they embedded and hoped to make immortal in the Constitution; without which the Constitution would not be worth the parchment on which it was written.

But I must not linger by the way, Mr. Speaker. What do these bills propose? The immediate object is to confiscate the property of the rebels. For what end? For punishment, is it not? If you strip these men of their property, it is not because they are innocent; although this bill does, in fact, confiscate the property of persons who may be guiltless of any offence: but the theory of the bill is to punish men for the crime of rebellion, or treason, or give it what name you will. The bill, indeed, recites, as an ulterior purpose, the payment of the expenses of the Rebellion. But there is no man on this floor so verdant as to suppose this means much. If the courts enforce the statute (I believe they will not), how much treasure can you wring from those States, poor at the best, but whom the close of this war will leave impoverished, seared, and swept as by fire? You might as well pasture your cattle on the Desert of Sahara. The land will indeed be left; but who will be your purchasers, when they know they must take at the best a doubtful title, but a sure, bitter, and lasting feud? The strife and hate growing out of the confiscations of the Revolution are scarcely yet appeased; and it was with these confiscations fresh in the memories of the framers of the Constitution that the limitation of the power of forfeiture was adopted. There never was a wilder dream than that of paying the expenses of the Rebellion with the fruits of confiscation.

The real object of the bill is punishment; the punishment of an offence clearly defined in the Constitution, of the highest offence known to the laws. The punishment is the forfeiture of the property of the offender. The forfeiture is to be established before judicial tribunals, and upon proof of the guilt of the owner. You have, then, these three elements; punishment — upon proof of the commission of crime — before a judicial tribunal. One element is wanting; one has been diligently excluded, — trial by jury. Human ingenuity has been exhausted to shut the door against it; and your bill is like Hamlet with the Prince of Denmark omitted by particular request. Here is the plain, imperative mandate of the Constitution, which he who runs may read: —

"The trial of all crimes, except in cases of impeachment, shall be by jury." — *Const.*, art. 3, sect. 2.

The property to which the bill applies is not, under the laws of nations, prize; it is not booty; it is not contraband of war; it is not enforced military contribution; it is not property used or employed in the war or in resistance to the laws, and therefore clearly to be distinguished from that covered by the statute of Aug. 6, 1861. It is private property outside of the conflict of arms; forfeited, not because it is the instrument of offence, but as a penalty for the crime of the owner. The disguise of the proceeding *in rem* is too thin and transparent. No lawyer, no man of common sense, will be deceived by it. The proceeding, in spirit, in substance, and in effect, is the punishment of treason by the forfeiture of a man's entire estate, real and personal, without trial by jury, and in utter disregard of the provision of the Constitution, which limits the forfeiture for treason to the life of the person attainted (art. 3, sect. 3).

Was there ever a balder contrivance to get around the plainest and most sacred provisions of the Constitution than this attempt to get a man's farm, his cattle and fodder, his plough, spade, and hoe, into a maritime court, and try them by the law of prize? With all respect for my excellent friends upon the committee, such a proposition "shocks our common sense" as well as our sense of justice and right. You make the plea of necessity, and necessity is the mother of invention; but do you expect to satisfy sensible men, when reason resumes its sway, that under a Constitution which defines treason to consist in levying war against the United States, which will not suffer the traitor to be condemned except by the judgment of his peers, and, when condemned, will not forfeit his estate except during his life, you can, by this proceeding *in rem*, without indictment, without trial by jury, without the proof of two witnesses (art. 3, sect. 3), for treason, for the act of levying war, deprive him of all his estate, real and personal, for life and in fee? Nay, more; and that, after he has thus been punished, without trial by jury, and by the loss of his whole estate, you can, for the same act of levying war, try him and hang him? To suggest a doubt, whether, after all, this is plain sailing under the flag of the Constitution, is to have too nice constitutional scruples!

I have touched but upon one or two legal objections to these bills. Their name is Legion; but I must hasten to a more minute examination of the bills themselves. I do not wish to say the bills are hastily drawn. If right in principle, defects of form, or want of detail, can be supplied. In attempting, however, legislation involving a new principle, or a new application of a principle, it is a pretty good test to let it be run through the machinery of a carefully drawn statute, and see how it works. I should have liked to have seen that test applied here.

Looking now to the general features of the confiscation bill, I desire the House to observe that the bill, though not in form, is, in substance and effect, retroactive. It takes effect from its passage. It applies to all acts committed after its passage. As there are whole districts, States even, where the law cannot be promulgated, and who will remain in ignorance of its passage, the law, as to them, will be *ex post facto*. They will neither know, nor have the means of knowing, of the existence of the penalty when the act is committed. Will you say it is their own fault? I beg you to consider, that since your protection has been lost, and until it is restored, there has been and can be no really free choice with the individual citizen whom he shall obey. What measure of punishment would you mete to a citizen of Jacksonville, who, after the withdrawal of your army, should yield to "the powers that be," though certainly *not* " ordained of God "?

I ask the attention of the House, and a just and humane people, if these words shall ever reach them, to the wide sweep of this bill. You would infer from the arguments of its friends, that the bill was to reach only the leaders and instigators of rebellion. How, if that were so, the limitation and the payment of the expenses of rebellion from confiscation would hang together, has not been explained. But the *fact* is far otherwise.

The first section includes several classes; and, first, all officers of the rebel army or navy, non-commissioned as well as commissioned. Officers of high rank should be included; but there is no sound reason whatever for going down to sergeants and corporals. The second, third, and fourth classes embrace persons who shall hold certain offices in the Confederate States, or any of them, including judges of the State Courts, and members of State Legislatures and conventions. In all these cases, the mere holding of the office is made the ground of confiscation, without regard to the manner in which the duties shall be discharged, or to whether those duties involve any active service against the National Government; men, it may be, whom the Rebellion found in office, and who continue in the regular exercise of their functions. Here, for example, is the judge of probate or surrogate of a county. Rebellion breaks out: men will die, and estates must be settled, and care had of widows and orphans. To visit this man with the confiscation of his estate, for continuing quietly to discharge his duties, is equally harsh and absurd.

The same remark applies, possibly with increased force, to persons embraced in the fifth class; those holding any office or agency under any of the States of the Confederacy, or any of the laws thereof, whether such office or agency be State or municipal in its name or character. Every justice of the peace, notary public, or town-clerk, treasurer, assessor, constable, overseer of the poor, undertaker even, must resign his functions, or become a pauper. The result, if successful, is a suspension of civil order; or, on the other hand, the severest punishment for a venial offence, if it be an offence.

The second section includes all persons who, being engaged in rebellion, or aiding and abetting it, shall not, within sixty days after proclamation from the President, desist, and return to their allegiance. Sixty days seems to be a reasonable notice; but, if the parties are in such condition that the notice cannot reach them, then it is not notice. What may be fairly and justly required is, that men shall return to their allegiance the moment they have reasonable assurance of permanent protection from the National Government. It is idle to look for it before such protection is possible. To ask a man in the interior of a cotton State to abjure the rebel Government and return to his allegiance, in the present condition of things, is to ask a moral impossibility. To confiscate his property for not doing so, is itself a crime.

A word upon another harsh feature of the bill. With respect to every person within its scope, and without the least discrimination as to degrees of guilt, a clean sweep of property is made. There is no exemption of necessary household furniture, or of provisions, or of tools of trade. Nothing is spared; the bed on which the wife sleeps, the cradle of the child, the pork, or flour-barrel. Taken in connection with the fact, that the bill declares that the President *shall* cause the seizure to be made, and not merely that he *may;* that provision is made for the sale of perishable property, and that none is made for the remission, in whole or part, of the forfeiture; and we cannot fail to understand the spirit in which the bill is conceived, or the impression it will not fail to make on the friends of this country abroad, who cannot fully appreciate the bitterness which civil conflict engenders; or, if they do, will not pardon statesmen for yielding to its influence. It is plain that the angel of mercy never found his way to the committee-room; or, if he went in with my friend from Kentucky [Mr. Mallory] or my friend from New Jersey [Mr. Cobb], he was politely bowed out, with the assurance that neither rebels, nor those dependent upon them, had any rights.

I ought, however, to add, Mr. Speaker, that, looking upon seizure and confiscation as a penalty for crime, treason, or rebellion, the President, under his general power of pardon, might remit the punishment. But then the other conclusion will follow, that, without trial by jury, no valid forfeiture can be effected.

The second bill, for the emancipation of the slaves of rebels, is much broader in its scope, including every person who shall engage in rebellion, or aid and abet it. The insertion of the word "wilfully," lawyers will see, does not affect the legal construction. There are considerations of humanity in favor of this bill, which do not apply to the first; but it is not restricted to slaves used in the Rebellion, and *no* form of judicial proceeding is provided. The constitutional objections apply to it with at least equal force.

That the bills before the House are in violation of the law of nations and of the Constitution, I cannot — I say it with all deference to others — I cannot entertain a doubt. My path of duty is plain. The duty of obedience to that Constitution was never more imperative than now. I am not disposed to deny, that I have for it a superstitious reverence. I have "worshipped it from my forefathers." In the school of rigid discipline by which we were prepared for it; in the struggles out of which it was born; the seven years of bitter conflict, and the seven darker years in which that conflict seemed to be fruitless of good; in the wisdom with which it was constructed and first administered and set in motion; in the beneficent Government it has secured for more than two generations; in the blessed influences it has exerted upon the cause of freedom and humanity the world over, I cannot fail to recognize the hand of a guiding and loving Providence. But not for the blessed memories of the past only do I cling to it. He must be blinded with excess of light, or with the want of it, who does not see, that to this nation, trembling on the verge of dissolution, it is the only possible bond of unity. With this conviction wrought into the very texture of my being, I believe I can appreciate this conflict, — can understand the necessity of using all the powers given by the Constitution for the suppression of this Rebellion. They are, as I believe, and as the progress of our arms attests, ample for the purpose. I do not, therefore, see the wisdom of violating or impairing the Constitution in the effort to save it, or of passing from the pestilent heresy of State secession to the equally fatal one of State suicide. The fruits of the first are anarchy and perpetual border war; of the second, the growth of military power, the loss of the centrifugal force of the States, the merging of the States in the central Government: a Republic in name and form; in substance and effect, a despotism.

Mr. Speaker, at a time like this, the individual is nothing; the country, every thing. He cannot truly serve or love his country who is anxious about himself. He cannot have a single eye to the welfare of the Republic, if both eyes are turned homeward. He cannot keep step to the music of the Union who is grinding fantasias for the village of Buncombe. One may desire, however, not to be wholly misunderstood. It has been said that I am opposed to any emancipation of the slaves of rebels. Nothing can be further from the truth. The first provision for emancipation, — that in the statute of Aug. 6, 1861, liberating all slaves employed in the Rebellion, — I drew with my own hand; believing now, as then, that it is valid and just. For the abolition of slavery in this District, for the interdiction of slavery in the Territories, for the new article of war forbidding the officers of the army to surrender fugitives from service, my votes are on record. I voted for the resolution recommended by the President for aid to the States in the work of gradual emancipation; though I could not fail to see that it was on the verge of authority, and must perhaps finally rest, like the purchase of Louisiana, upon general consent. My views of the power of the Commander-in-chief on the subject of emancipation are fully stated in remarks submitted to the House on the 10th of April. I will not repeat them. They are ample for any emergency. In the bill I introduced " for the more effectual suppression of the Rebellion," but which, in the present temper of the House, I thought it useless to press, I have indicated a practical method by which the slaves of rebels may be emancipated, as the penalty for crime, upon conviction or default of the offender. But, Mr. Speaker, I have kept my eye steadily upon the end for which this war is waged, — the only end for which it can be justified, — the integrity of the Union. I have firmly resisted, and shall continue firmly to resist, every effort, open or disguised, to convert this war for the

Union into a war for emancipation, at the risk — no, not at the risk, for the words do not express what I mean or feel, with the moral certainty — of defeating the purpose for which the war was begun. With these convictions, it is scarcely necessary to say, I cordially approve the course of President Lincoln in modifying the proclamation of General Frémont, and declaring null and void the order of General Hunter. For the wisdom and patriotism which have thus far marked the course of this magistrate, he has my respect and gratitude.

A word upon the policy and wisdom of these measures. A great work has been done by this nation. It is easy to find fault. In operations upon so large a scale, requiring so many agencies, mistakes and blunders will be made. But a just criticism, looking upon the work as a whole, cannot fail to commend the patriotism of the people and the energy of the Government. I know it has been prettily said, that we have prosecuted this war upon " a rose-water policy." I do not know that I fully comprehend what is meant; but probably the rebels, in view of that long blockade, with the fresh memories of Port Royal, Newbern, Pulaski, Donelson, Pea Ridge, Shiloh, the Lower Mississippi, and Yorktown, and the ever-tightening folds of the constriction, might say with Juliet, the

"Rose
By any other name would smell as sweet."

Our armies and navies are victorious. The war *seems* to be drawing to a close. There is reasonable ground to *hope*, that, before the next session of Congress, the power of the Rebellion will be broken, and the sword have substantially done its work. But I cannot conceal from myself that our great difficulties lie beyond the conflict of arms. It is the part of wise courage to look them calmly in the face, to gauge them, and gird up our loins to meet them. Action will be needed, not words; judgment, not passion. Unless there be calm and fearless statesmanship, your victories will have been won in vain; a statesmanship that honors and respects the people, but is willing to abide its sober second thought.

Civil wars, like family feuds, have been fierce, bitter, and unrelenting. The bitterness and ferocity manifested towards us by the rebels cannot but arouse the spirit of retaliation, and thirst for vengeance. If we yield to the fierce temptation, the war will become one of extermination. Thus far, while prosecuting the war with vigor, we have shown the moderation and humanity becoming a great people. I pray we may continue in this course. There is wisdom in the fable of the sun and the north wind. There is power in forbearance, in magnanimity, in obedience to the law we seek to enforce, in the spirit of forgiveness, in the "mercy which seasons justice." Christ knew what is in man: the gospel is not a lie. There never was a juster war than that which we are waging. It is strictly a war of self-defence, the defence of a free and beneficent Government against traitors in arms against her. But we may not forget, that, to those in the Southern States who believe in the right of secession, this war cannot but wear the aspect of a war of invasion and subjugation. This terrible mistake may account for their bitterness, though it is no palliation for their barbarities.

Mr. Speaker, upon no subject has there been more or looser declamation than on the causes of this Rebellion. At one moment, we are assured that slavery is the one great criminal; at the next, that it was brought about by the fraud, falsehood, and violence of a few unprincipled leaders.

Passing this subject now with the remark, that masses of men are not easily moved, that civil convulsions are fed by deeper fires, I ask your attention to two facts which seem to be clearly established. The first is, that, when the acts of secession were passed, the majority of the people of the revolting States, with the exception of South Carolina, were loyal to the Union; and the second is, that to-day their feelings are changed, their loyalty turned to treason, and love to hate. Passion is eloquent; but do not content yourselves with bitter denunciation. Pause, I beseech and adjure you, and inquire what is the cause.

The war brought to their homes and firesides will account for much; but do you not believe that a conviction has been settling down into the minds of men, who at the beginning of our troubles were loyal, that these extreme measures point to some other end than the restoration of the Union with the rights of the States preserved; that they mean subjugation and reconstruction " by permission of the military power, and not before "? Once committed to this policy, once afloat on this sea of revolution, neither you nor I may live to reach the haven of Union and peace.

If these measures shall be finally adopted, I pray God I may prove a false prophet, and that " out of this nettle danger we may pluck the flower safety;" that his strength may be manifested in our weakness; and that he may overrule all our errors and shortcomings for the good of our beloved country.

THE TREASURY-NOTE BILL.

IN THE HOUSE OF REPRESENTATIVES, FEB. 6, 1862.

The House being in Committee of the Whole on the State of the Union, and having under consideration the Treasury-note Bill, Mr. THOMAS said, —

Mr. CHAIRMAN, — I am anxious to vote for some measure for the speedy relief of the Government. I have listened with care to the whole debate, with the hope that the difficulties which had occurred to my own mind might be relieved. Nay, more: I have diligently sought to convince myself that it was in the power of Congress to pass this bill, including the provision making the treasury notes legal tender for all public and private debts. I have wished to see also that the bill could be passed, and the good faith of this Government maintained. I have failed upon both of these points; and, with the indulgence of the Committee, will state briefly some of the reasons which will lead me to vote against the bill as it now stands.

The question at the threshold of the discussion is that of legal power, the competency of Congress to pass the bill. Congress has upon this subject the powers given to it by the Constitution. This is a Government of specific powers, supreme in their sphere, but the sphere confessedly limited.

We look to the Constitution to see if the power is given. We do not say the power is not denied, and therefore exists; but that it is not granted, and therefore does not exist. The powers granted are express or implied, are given in terms, or are the reasonable inferences from the express grants. Now, it is conceded that there is no express power given to Congress to make the notes or bills of the Government legal tender. There is a power given to Congress upon the subject-matter. It has the power " to coin money, regulate the value thereof and of foreign coins."

These words, "to coin money," have a plain and obvious meaning. The only coinage is that of the metals, " hard money." To coin money, and regulate the value thereof, is to fix its legal value, the value for which it is to be received as an equivalent in commerce and in discharge of obligations and contracts. This constitutional power of coinage was first executed by the statute of 1792, and that statute has a provision making the coins legal tender; but there can be no doubt, that, whenever money is coined by Government under the Constitution, it becomes *ipso facto* legal tender. But, whether legislation be necessary to carry the provision into effect or not, it is too plain for argument, that the power to coin money and regulate its value is the power to say for what value it shall be received.

There being no express power in the Constitution to make these treasury notes a legal tender, is such a power to be reasonably inferred from any of the express powers? Before answering this question, two things are to be observed.

The first is, that, there being an express grant of power upon this subject of the coining of money and fixing its legal value, we should not reasonably expect to find an additional power on the same subject given by implication. The expression of the one would ordinarily be the exclusion of the other. The second thing to be noted is, that it appears by the debates of the Constitutional Convention, and by the note of Mr. Madison, that this subject was before the convention, and that a grant of power to emit bills of credit, with the apparent purpose of making them legal tender, was refused. — Pages 1343–46.

It is said that the power to make these notes a legal tender is a reasonable implication from the power "to regulate commerce with foreign nations, among the States, and with the Indian tribes." The argument is, and it is entitled to consideration, that money is one of the great instruments of commerce, as much so as the ship; and that the power to regulate the principal thing is the power to regulate its instrumentalities. I confess, that, at first, this view of the question impressed me. But further reflection has satisfied me it is not sound. If the Constitution were otherwise silent upon the subject, the implication would doubtless be a strong one.

But the Constitution has spoken; has indicated what shall be money under its provisions, and the power of Congress over it.

Again: the practical construction of the Constitution has been, that no such power existed. Though the exigencies of the Government have heretofore been great, the experiment has never been tried; nor, so far as I know, ever before suggested.

Of the three great statesmen whose minds have been given to this subject of the currency, and the power of the National Government over it, no one has asserted the existence of this power. Mr. Madison and Mr. Webster have expressly denied its existence. Mr. Webster had, of all our statesmen, except perhaps Mr. Hamilton, the strongest convictions of the necessity of a national currency, and of the duty of Congress to control it; but, on the want of power in Congress to make any thing but coin legal tender, his language is clear, firm, and unequivocal. He says, —

"But if we understand by currency the *legal money* of the country, and that which constitutes a legal tender for debts, and is the statute measure of value, then, undoubtedly, nothing is included but gold and silver. *Most unquestionably, there is no legal tender, and there can be no legal tender, in this country, under the authority of this Government or any other, but gold and silver, either the coinage of our own mints, or foreign coins at rates regulated by Congress.* This is a constitutional principle, perfectly plain, and of the very highest importance. The States are expressly prohibited from making any thing but gold and silver a tender in payment of debts; and although no such express prohibition is applied to Congress, yet, as Congress has no power granted to it in this respect but to coin money and to regulate the value of foreign coins, it clearly has no power to substitute paper or any thing else for coin as a tender in payment of debts and in discharge of contracts. Congress has exercised this power fully in both its branches. It has coined money, and still coins it; it has regulated the value of foreign coins, and still regulates their value. *The legal tender, therefore, the constitutional standard of value, is established, and cannot be overthrown. To overthrow it would shake the whole system.*

"But, if the Constitution knows only gold and silver as a legal tender, does it follow that the Constitution cannot tolerate the voluntary circulation of bank-notes, convertible into gold and silver at the will of the holder, as part of the actual money of the country? Is a man not only to be entitled to demand gold and silver for every debt, but is he, or should he be, obliged to demand it in all cases? Is it, or should Government make it, unlawful to receive pay in any thing else? Such a notion is too absurd to be seriously treated. The constitutional *tender* is the thing to be preserved; and it ought to be preserved sacredly, under all circumstances. — *Webster's Works*, vol. iv. p. 271.

Again he says, —

"I am certainly of opinion, then, that gold and silver, at rates fixed by Congress, constitute the legal standard of value in this country; *and that neither Congress nor any State has authority to establish any other standard or to displace this.*" — *Ibid.*, vol. iv. p. 280.

This is good law and solid sense.

There is, Mr. Chairman, another difficulty in inferring from the power of Congress to regulate commerce the power to make treasury notes legal tender, which has not been adverted to. It is this: The power given to Congress is to regulate commerce " *among* the States." Now, it is clear in principle, and well settled as authority, that the provision does not extend to and include the *internal* commerce of the States. This power is reserved to the States themselves (Gibbons *vs.* Ogden, 12 Wheaton, 1). Looking at this power to make these notes a legal tender as incident to the power of Congress to regulate commerce, the power of the incident cannot extend beyond the power of the principal. This bill clearly includes a commerce over which we have no control. It is scarcely necessary to say that this internal commerce would include nine out of ten of all the bargains that are made.

It has been said, that, under the power to " borrow

money on the credit of the United States," we have the power to make the securities given for borrowed money legal tender; that is to say, under the power to *borrow*, we have the power to *create*.

It would seem to be a sufficient answer to this position to say, that, if the Government had the power to make its notes money by its superscription only, there would be no great need to borrow.

It has been argued, that because the power is denied to the States to make " any thing but gold and silver a tender in payment of debts," and is not denied in terms to Congress, it therefore exists in Congress. To this position the answer is twofold: First, that the express power has been given to Congress of coining *money*, and regulating its value; the value for which it is to be received in the marts of commerce in the payment of debts or the measure of damages. The money so coined is the only money known to the Constitution. The Constitution never confounds, as does this bill, money with the promise to pay money, the shadow with the substance, the sign with the thing signified. The second and obvious answer is, that the power, not being delegated to Congress, is reserved, under article ten of the Amendments, to the people. The people, acting in the light of their own terrible experience, would neither give the power to Congress, nor permit its exercise by the States. If the power to make money of paper is an attribute of sovereignty, as the friends of this bill aver, the attribute yet rests securely in the bosom of the sovereign. The people have not parted with this power of evil.

Mr. Chairman, though the legal question has not been judicially settled, I feel compelled to say that the weight of reasoning and authority is strongly against the validity of the clause making the treasury notes legal tender. If the validity of the provision be doubtful even, and it becomes, as it inevitably would, the subject of contest and litigation in the courts, the effect upon the credit of the paper will, in my judgment, be worse than if the tender clause had been wholly omitted.

I have a word or two to say upon the *justice* of this clause of the bill.

To make these notes legal tender for debts, private and public, contracted before the passage of the bill, seems to me a clear breach of good faith. Debts are obligations or promises to pay money, the only money known to the Constitution and laws; the universal equivalent having not merely intrinsic value, but being the measure and standard of value. Paper is *not money*. The draft, bill, or note, is the mere *sign:* money is the *thing signified*. Said John Locke, " Men in their bargains contract, not for denominations or sounds, but for the *intrinsic value.*"

This bill, Mr. Chairman, changes the condition and practically impairs the obligation of every existing contract to pay money. When the contract to pay money matures, this bill compels the creditor to take for his debt, not money, not even paper convertible into money on demand, but the promise of Government to pay at a future day uncertain. It is a perfect answer of the creditor to this proposition to say, " That is not my agreement: a matured debt is not paid by a promise to pay."

But further: the faith of the contract is broken, because the creditor is not paid in gold or silver, nor in that which is equivalent to gold and silver. He neither gets the coin, nor its value in any form; the money, nor the money's worth. Take, for example, one of the treasury notes issued under the act of July 17, payable in three years, with interest at the rate of seven and three-tenths per cent semi-annually. When the interest is due, the Government is asked to pay. It offers its note convertible into stock worth now eighty-eight cents on the dollar. The holder of the note reads the ninth section of the statute of July: —

"*And be it further enacted*, That the faith of the United States is hereby solemnly pledged for the payment of the interest, and redemption of the principal, of the loan authorized by this act."

If the lender had understood that by payment of interest was meant the giving another note, payable at the pleasure of the Government, would the loan have been effected? When, by compulsion, he takes your note, and converts it into stock, worth, it may be, eighty-eight or seventy-five cents on a dollar, will he go away with the conviction, that the faith of the United States, so solemnly pledged, has been as solemnly redeemed? Will he not feel that faith without works is dead? No craft of logic or of rhetoric can disguise the real nature of that transaction. If we feel stain like a wound, that wound is immedicable. Take from us, Mr. Chairman, our property, houses, and lands, — they cannot be devoted to a nobler cause: but, in God's name, leave us the consciousness of integrity; leave us our self-respect. Delays may be inevitable; but we will pay the uttermost farthing.

If the provision of the bill be not just, it is, of course, impolitic. It will wound our credit vitally. It will defeat the very end it was designed to accomplish. That credit can only be maintained as individuals or as a nation by the utmost fidelity to our engagements; by keeping our promises as we keep our oaths, — registered in heaven.

No matter what may be the resources of the country; no matter what may be its actual wealth, or its capacity to acquire it: your creditor has no lien upon your property. He can make no levy upon your lands or goods. If you refuse or fail to pay, he is without remedy. After all, his sole reliance must be upon your good faith. In the keeping of that is his security and your credit. And you cannot afford the experiment of giving him paper when you promised him money. It will cost you, in the long-run, even more than it will cost him.

This provision of the bill, in the nature of a forced loan, is itself a confession of weakness. It seeks to compel credit for the reason that it does not come spontaneously. It assumes that force is necessary to uphold that which must stand on its own legs, or cannot stand at all. Credit is faith, is trust, is confidence. If you faithfully keep your promises; if by taxation you avail yourselves of all the resources of the country for the salvation of the country; if you keep always in view the end for which this conflict is waged; if, in seeking to enforce the Constitution and the laws, you show a readiness yourselves to obey the Constitution and the laws, you will win credit: you cannot command or enforce it. It will follow in the footsteps of rectitude: you cannot drive it before you. You may by this bill say that paper is money; give the same name to things vitally different. The essential difference will be none the less clearly perceived and strongly felt. It is no want of respect to say to you, You cannot change the nature of things.

The friends of this feature of the bill, Mr. Chairman, admit the reluctance with which they assent to it. The only ground of defence is its necessity; that no alternative is left to us. I respect their motives: I cannot see the necessity.

We have spent a great deal of money in this war, and have wasted a great deal. But we are not impoverished. What we have spent is trivial in comparison to what is left. The amount up to this time will not exceed two years of surplus profits. It is not more than one thirty-second part of our whole property. Not a dollar of tax has been raised; and yet we are talking of national bankruptcy, and launching upon a paper currency. I may be very dull; but I cannot see the necessity or the wisdom of such a course.

Gentlemen who appreciate the perils of this step would relieve themselves and us by the assurance, that the amount of paper to be issued is restricted within safe bounds. These barriers are easily surmounted. It is the first step which costs. The descent has always been easy. The difficulty is return. The experience of mankind shows the danger in entering upon this path; that boundaries are fixed only to be overrun, promises made only to be broken. Human nature remains essentially the same. We are neither wiser nor better than our fathers. The theatre changes, but not the actors or the drama. In speaking of emissions of paper-money, Hamilton, the greatest of our statesmen, and the most sagacious of our financiers, says,—

> "The wisdom of the Government will be shown in never trusting itself with the use of so seducing and dangerous an expedient. In times of tranquillity, it might have no ill consequence; it might even perhaps be managed in a way to be productive of good: but, in great and trying emergencies, there is almost a moral certainty of its becoming mischievous. The stamping of paper is an operation so much easier than the laying of taxes, that a government in the practice of paper emissions would rarely fail, in any such emergency, to indulge itself too far in the employment of that resource, to avoid, as much as possible, one less auspicious to present popularity." — *Hamilton's Works*, vol. iii. p. 124.

The ordinary check, the only effectual check, in the issue of paper for currency, the security of the public against excess in its issue, is that the excess will be returned upon the banks for gold and silver. A certain amount is needed for the purposes of the currency. When that point is reached, the paper begins to decline, the gold and silver are demanded, and the issues of paper are contracted. If there be an excess of gold and silver, it will right itself by exportation, or find its way into the arts. To the issue of this paper there is no natural check or restraint. When it begins to depreciate, the necessity is at once created for increasing the issues; public distrust is increased; and this again leads to still further depreciation and to still larger issues. The process of decline is easy, natural, inevitable.

The results are the familiar things of history: prices expand; "new ways to pay old debts" are opened; the hearts of men glow as with new wine. But all is unreal: not a farthing is added to the substantial wealth of the country. The seeming prosperity, "having no root in itself, abides but for a time." The contraction and depression are as rapid and as great as were the rise and exaltation; and men come down from the cloud-land to mourn over blighted hopes and broken promises and wasted fortunes, and to feel soberly that the laws of nature and of Providence are stronger than the laws or the hopes of men.

One thing to be noted is, that the heaviest share of the burden always falls upon labor. Never were wiser words than those of Mr. Webster: "Of all contrivances for cheating the laboring classes of mankind, none has been more effectual than that which deluded them with paper-money. Ordinary tyranny, oppression, excessive taxation, — these bear lightly on the *mass* of the community, compared with fraudulent currencies and the robberies committed by depreciated paper."

A word, Mr. Chairman, and I will relieve the patience of the Committee. It has been said that coming generations ought to bear a large part of the expenses of this war, and that we may therefore justly create a large public debt. A debt will doubtless be created; but the burdens of the war ought, as far as possible, to fall upon the men of this generation. We are but keeping in repair the structure of our fathers, not building a new one. This expense should be borne mainly by the tenants for life, and not by the heirs. For the discharge of this duty, we need four things: unity of purpose, energy of action, the largest possible taxation, and the severest possible retrenchment.

RECOGNITION OF LIBERIA AND HAYTI.

HOUSE OF REPRESENTATIVES, JUNE 3, 1862.

Mr. Speaker, — After the excellent speech of my friend and colleague who introduced this bill [Mr. Gooch], any thing like elaborate argument is unnecessary; but I desire to state very briefly the reasons which will induce me to vote for it, and especially for that portion of it which recognizes the independence and establishes diplomatic relations with the Republic of Liberia. My interest in this State of Liberia was an early and strong one. Whether we look at its past history or at its probable future destiny, it is among the most interesting of modern States. The Government and people of this country sustain to it a near and intimate relation. It was planted by our care. It is the fruit of the labors, the sacrifices, and the prayers of wise and good men among us. Its existence is a slight atonement for the cruelty, the perfidy, the injustice, which by us, as by other Christian States, have been lavished on the continent of Africa, the land of God's sunshine and of man's hate. It is the outpost of her civilization; the opened gateway through which the arts of peace, social order and Christianity, may enter, and gain a permanent foothold.

That Liberia is of sufficient commercial importance to justify the institution of diplomatic relations with her, has been clearly shown. Every year will develop, quicken, and enlarge this commerce, if we choose to watch over and protect it. Our interests lie in the path of our duty.

I am not prepared, Mr. Speaker, to say that the recognition of an independent State, although it may have sufficient power to maintain both commercial and political relations with us, is a matter of absolute duty under the law of nations. It is, perhaps, what moral writers would call a duty of imperfect obligation. But in respect to this colony, and to the men who have gone out from this country to plant and train it up, there has been from the beginning an assurance of the assistance, the counsel, and the protection of this Government; and the recognition on our part is required by good faith as well as sound policy. Other nations have preceded us in the recognition. It was our duty and privilege to have been first.

If there were no elements entering into the discussion of this question but the relations which the Republic of Liberia holds to-day to the rest of the civilized world, the importance of its commerce, of its capacity to maintain, as it has for years maintained, an independent Government, with the fact that two of the most powerful nations of the earth have already recognized its independence, there would have been no discussion of this bill. The only ground of objection is, that that State has been planted and built up by an inferior race of men.

I have no desire to enter into the question of the relative capacity of races; but, if the inferiority of the African race were established, the inference as to our duty would be very plain. If this colony has been built up by an inferior race of men, it has a yet stronger claim on our countenance, recognition, and, if need be, protection. The instincts of the human mind and heart concur with the policy of men and governments to help and protect the weak. To a child or to a woman I am to show a degree of forbearance, kindness, gentleness even, which I am not necessarily to extend to my equal.

But, sir, this colony is founded by black men, and not by white. If my friend from Ohio [Mr. Cox] had introduced a resolution that all commerce should be interdicted with the "Black Sea," I should not have been more surprised. I am not aware that the law of nations or the comity of nations recognizes the distinction between black and white men; and it is rather late to attempt to ingraft it upon the code.

Upon the question of admission to the society of nations, the law looks to the capacity of the State to maintain self-government, its capacity for political and commercial relations, and its general conformity to the usages and manners of civilized States.

Mr. Cox. I ask my friend from Massachusetts, whether the law of nations does not apply now, without this recognition of Liberia and Hayti; and whether we can make the law of nations apply by passing this act of Congress.

Mr. Thomas. I will answer the question with pleasure. If, within the rules of the law of nations, the

States of Liberia and Hayti are now independent powers, then it is plain, that, by this resolution, we recognize only an existing status or fact. I do understand, Mr. Speaker, that the Republics of Liberia and Hayti to-day belong to the society of States: but what we have to pass upon now is, whether this nation will affirm their admission, and hold with them commercial and diplomatic relations; and, if so, to what extent? If the position of my friend from Ohio be right, as I dare say it is, that they are already independent States, then we are doing no harm, surely, in recognizing and confirming what other nations have done.

But the precise question is, whether we can fairly regard the fact of the color of the race by which the State has been built up and maintained in deciding this matter. My position is, that by no just application of the principles of international law can that distinction be made. Nor is the question before us a question of taste, much less of narrow prejudice. The question, whether a minister from a foreign State is to be received, is to be determined on higher grounds. Personal objections are sometimes interposed. Nations decline to receive as ministers persons whose residence would, by the laws or usages of the country, be inadmissible; but I am not aware of rejection from the hue of the skin.

President Roberts, of the Republic of Liberia, was here some years ago. Many gentlemen will recollect him. No man who had seen him and conversed with him, or who knew any thing of his character, would for a moment object to his appearing here as a minister of that republic to this Government. Such a man would not infect even the *pure* air of the capital, nor would he be much cowed by the presence of a *superior* race!

But, as I have before said, Mr. Speaker, this is not a question of taste. It is a question of the fair application of the principles of international comity; it is a question, whether this people have so built up a State as to have a fair claim to the recognition of this Government.

It is said, Mr. Speaker, that if we are to make this recognition, and to establish these relations, this is not the *proper time* to do so. Why not the proper time? This State has been in a condition to maintain these relations with us for a number of years. But a portion of the representation of this country is absent! Not by our fault, Mr. Speaker. Congress is not to cease to exercise the functions of legislation because men or States are not here to attend to the public interests. If they choose to forego their *privileges*, we must, nevertheless, discharge our *duties*. If a few of our friends here should absent themselves from our discussions, we should not consider ourselves under any obligation whatever, on that account, to give up the ordinary work of legislation. I cannot be influenced by the consideration, that States have neglected the duty imposed upon them by the Constitution. We are to determine this question upon the same considerations and from the same motives as if this Rebellion had not occurred.

Mr. Speaker, so far from being deterred from this recognition by this question of race, I would make this recognition the sooner because it was some measure of atonement to a grossly wronged and injured race. While

I am ready on every occasion, in this House and elsewhere, to recognize and affirm the rightful power of the States over their domestic institutions, I am not to conceal from myself the fact, that, from the beginning of the history of the country to this hour, our course as a people towards that race has been one of cruelty and injustice.

There are two things in this country which are often confounded, but which are not very nearly akin, — hatred of the slaveholder, and love of the slave; abstract love of the race, and practical love of the men who compose it. I frankly confess, Mr. Speaker, that I have never been more grieved on this floor, than when I saw gentlemen, who during the whole winter have been ventilating their rhetoric on the wrongs of slavery and of the race subject to its iron rule, deliberately record their votes against extending to a man of color, whatever his capacity or ability or fidelity, the power or right to serve the Government, even in the humble capacity of carrying the mail on his shoulders, or on horseback, if he could make a horse contract. Rhetoric is beautiful; but it is not meat or bread or raiment, or the right to work for meat or bread or raiment.

This by the way. It cannot escape observation, Mr. Speaker, that our relations with the States of Liberia and Hayti may soon assume new importance. As the result of the legislation of the last session, and as the *natural, inevitable* result of this war, the number of free persons of color in this country will be greatly increased. The Free States are barring their doors against them. Abstract love is simpler and easier than practical. They may feel the necessity of going out from the house of political and social bondage. The doors of Liberia and Hayti are open to receive them. Our sympathy, our aid, our protection, ought to go with them; and intimate political and commercial relations will be essential for those ends.

A gentle hint, and I will trespass no longer on the time and courtesy of my colleague, who is to close the debate. Much has been said, justly said, on this floor, of men of one idea. One idea does not make a statesman, more than one swallow makes a summer. We do not admire the spring that can' fill but one bucket, the mill that will grind but one grist, the quiver with one arrow, the hen with one chicken. Again: one idea or feeling may be so strong as to give color to all the rest. That idea or feeling may be ardent *aversion* to the negro race, as well as ardent *love* for it. In shunning Scylla, we may touch Charybdis.

DEATH OF HON. GOLDSMITH F. BAILEY.

HOUSE OF REPRESENTATIVES, MAY 15, 1862.

MY colleagues, Mr. Speaker, have assigned to me the duty of announcing to the House the death of one of our number — Hon. Goldsmith F. Bailey, at his home in Fitchburg, Mass. — on the 8th instant.

The story of his life is a brief and manly one. He was born on the 17th of July, 1823, in Westmoreland, N.H.; a State that has given to her sisters so many of her jewels, and yet always kept her casket full and sparkling. An orphan at the age of two, he was thrown wholly upon his own resources at the age of twelve. What we ordinarily call education (schooling) was finished substantially at the age of sixteen. But he early discovered that the only true culture is self-culture; the only true development, self-development; that in the sweat of a man's own face he must eat the bread of knowledge; and that in the school of narrow fortune and of early struggle are often to be found the most invigorating disciplines and the wisest teachers.

At the age of sixteen, he began to learn the art of printing. We need but glance at our history, or look around us at either end of the Capitol, to learn, that as printing is the most encyclopedic of arts, so the printing-office is among the best places of instruction. In diffusing knowledge, the pupil acquires it; and, in preparing the instruments for educating others, educates himself. I have revered the art from my forefathers, as Paul would have said; and mine, therefore, may be a partial judgment: but some of the best educated men it has been my pleasure to know received their degrees at the printer's college.

Mr. Bailey, having learned his art, was for some time the associate printer, publisher, and editor of a country newspaper; a business, I suspect, not very lucrative or attractive. It did not fill the measure of his hopes; and, in 1845, he left the printing-office for the study of the law. He pursued his studies in the office of Messrs. Torrey and Wood of Fitchburg, sound lawyers and most estimable men. Their appreciation of their student was such, that upon his admission to the bar in December, 1848, he was received into the firm as a partner.

Mr. Bailey had been in the practice of his profession some thirteen years before his election to this House. A leading position at the bar in New England is seldom attained in thirteen years, and especially at a bar, which, even from days before the Revolution, has been so eminent as that of the county of Worcester. But Mr. Bailey had acquired high rank among his brethren, and by courteous manners, careful learning, sound judgment, and sterling integrity, had secured the respect of the people and of courts and juries.

His public life was very brief. In 1856, he was elected a representative in the Legislature of Massachusetts; and, in 1858 and 1860, was a member of the State Senate. In this new field of labor he was eminently successful; and, in his second year in the Senate, it may be fairly said, there was no man in the body in whom his colleagues or the public reposed more confidence.

The ability and fidelity with which he discharged these high duties attracted the attention and won the regard of the people of his district; and in November, 1860, in a canvass warmly contested by an able and popular man, he was elected to this House.

He took his seat at the extra session in July. But over his new and expanded horizon the night was already shutting down. The hand of death was laid visibly upon him. You could hear the very rustling of his wings.

He came back in December apparently a little better. It was but the glow of sunset, — the flickering of the flame before it goes out. He lost strength from day to day, and at last went home to die, — to realize the Spanish benediction, "May you die among your kindred!" and, what is of infinitely greater moment, the divine benediction, "Blessed are the dead who die in the Lord."

To our narrow vision, Mr. Speaker, such a life seems imperfect, such a death premature, — to wrestle with adverse fortune, as Jacob with the angel, until you wrest from it its blessing; to struggle through youth and early manhood; to reach the threshold of mature life, of usefulness, and of honor, and to sink weary and exhausted before the open door.

It *is* a narrow view, Mr. Speaker, which a serene trust in God and in his infinite wisdom and infinite goodness at once dispels. We wipe the mist from our eyes, and see that all is well. In the presence and with the consciousness of an immortal life, what matters it whether much or little be spent this side the veil, provided, as with our departed brother, it is well spent?

Mr. Speaker, death is busy everywhere around us. The accomplished jurist, the pure patriot, the statesman wise and good, passes away in the sabbath stillness.* Amid the thunders of artillery rocking like a cradle land and sea, amid fire and smoke, the shrieks of the wounded, the groans of the dying, the wail of defeat, and the shouts of triumph, the angel-reapers are gathering in fields seemingly not white for the harvest. The flower of our youth, the beauty of our Israel, is slain in our high places. The victories in this holy struggle for national life and "liberty in law" are sealed with our most precious blood. Yet in this hour of chastened triumph, of mingled joy and sadness, that tranquil death in a far-off New-England home comes very nigh to us with its solemn, I trust not unheeded warning, "Be ye also ready."

I offer the following resolutions: —

Resolved, That the House has heard with profound sorrow the announcement of the death of Hon. Goldsmith F. Bailey, a member of this House from the Ninth Congressional District of the State of Massachusetts.

---

* Samuel F. Vinton.

Resolved, That this House tenders to the widow and relatives of the deceased the expression of its deep sympathy in this afflicting bereavement.

Resolved, That the Clerk of this House communicate to the widow of the deceased a copy of these resolutions.

Resolved (as a further mark of respect), That a copy of these resolutions be communicated to the Senate, and that the House do now adjourn.

CASE OF THE "TRENT."

HOUSE OF REPRESENTATIVES, JAN. 7, 1862.

I DESIRE to say a word upon the subject to which the motion* refers.

Mr. Speaker, the surrender is made, the thing done. In the presence of great duties, we have no time for the luxury of grief. Complaint of the Government would be useless, if not groundless. It was too much to ask of it to take another war on its hands. Possibly the elaborate and ingenious argument of the Secretary might have been spared. The matter was in a nutshell; the answer, in a word: "Take them. There are duties lying nearer to us. We can wait."

But we are not called upon, Mr. Speaker, to say that the demand of England was manly or just. It was unmanly and unjust. It was a demand, which, in view of her history, of the rights she had always claimed and used as a belligerent power, of the principles which her greatest of jurists, Lord Stowell, had embedded in the law of nations, England was fairly estopped to make. But I rely on no estoppel: I pause not to inquire as to the consistency of England, or how far she is influenced by the consideration that she is now a

---

* The motion to refer the message of the President, transmitting the correspondence on this case, to the Committee on Foreign Affairs.

neutral power, and we are in a struggle for national life; or to express surprise that her belligerent doctrines, so suddenly become obsolete, have been swept as cobwebs from her path. This is a question of legal right; and, as such, I will look it in the face. We may feel compelled to make concessions: we will ask none. The claim of England is that the "Trent" was pursuing a lawful and innocent voyage, and that the taking from her of Messrs. Mason and Slidell was an affront to the British flag and a violation of international law.

The legal questions involved are simple, and may be briefly and plainly stated.

Had we the right of visitation and search? There is no controversy on this point. Nothing is better settled in the law of nations than the right of a belligerent to visit and search the vessel of a neutral for contraband of war, or to ascertain if she is employed in the transportation of military persons or despatches of the enemy. Was the "Trent" so employed? How is that question to be settled? The obvious answer is by the *existing* law of nations. The question is, not what rule *ought now* to be adopted, but what is the *existing* rule? New rules are guides for future action, not tests of the past. The common law of nations, like that of England and of this country, is, to a large extent, a law of precedents. These precedents are, however, of weight and authority for the *principles involved* in their determination, and not merely in cases where all the facts are identical. The whole body of the common law is the result of this distinction. It could not otherwise be a science or intelligent rule of action. The province of courts, of jurists, and of statesmen, is to apply settled principles to new combinations of facts. From the mass of authorities let us extract the *principles* applicable to the case.

1. The fair result of the authorities, and especially of the English authorities, is that the carrying of the despatches of a belligerent is a violation of neutrality, the penalty of which is not only the seizure of the despatches, but the seizure and confiscation of the vehicle which carries them, if the carriage be with the knowledge or complicity of the owner or master.

2. The rule includes the official despatches of the enemy, whether relating to civil or military affairs.

3. The form in which the despatches are borne is immaterial. They may be oral as well as written, embodied as well as upon parchment. The mischief is the same. The reason of the rule covers the substance, which is the thing sent.

4. If the neutral is serving the belligerent, doing his work, the fact that the despatches, living or written, were taken at a neutral port, and that, at the time of the seizure, the vessel was going from one neutral port to another, is material only upon the question of the forfeiture of the vessel, and as tending to show that the despatches were taken without the privity of master or owner. The result to be effected — the aid to the one belligerent, and the injury to the other — is the same. The sanction of the exception would be the constant evasion, the practical suspension, of the rule itself.

The substance of the whole matter is this: By carrying the despatches of the enemy, in whatever form embodied, the greatest possible service may be done to one belligerent, and the greatest possible injury to another.

If, then, the "Trent" had been brought in for adjudication, and had been condemned, England could not have said, that, *as matter of law*, the condemnation was wrong. She might and would have said, that, as matter of courtesy, our officers should have foreborne the exercise of their extreme right, and have suffered the vessel, the other passengers and cargo, to proceed on the voyage.

We might well have said, that, from the beginning, it had been the policy of this Government to enlarge and strengthen the rights of neutrals; to free neutral commerce from every unnecessary restraint; that especially had this been the case with respect to the treating of *persons* as within the rule of contraband of war. We might have shown with what anxiety we had sought to limit the rule on this point "*to soldiers in the actual service of the enemy;*" that in our treaties with France, in our treaties with Mexico and the South-American States, we had inserted this important exception to, and limitation of, the rule of international law; in all cases, however, providing that the limitation should not extend to those nations with which we had no such treaty; of which England was one. We might have well said, that the propriety of this limitation is every day becoming more apparent; that the introduction of steam into navigation had brought nations into closer proximity, and into more frequent and regular intercourse; that the wants of modern commerce and modern culture had made mail-routes as necessary on the sea as on the land; and that we ought to remove all obstructions from the pathway of these messengers of civilization and of peace. We might have said, We will gladly assent to such modifications of the law of nations as shall meet and satisfy these wants; the modifications most clearly demanded being, that no persons shall be deemed within the principle of contraband of war but soldiers in service; and that, when hostile despatches are taken from neutral mail-steamers, the claims of humanity and the interests of the commercial world shall be respected, and the vessel be permitted to proceed on its voyage without unnecessary delay, — the legality of the seizure being determined without the presence of the ship.

As to this case, we stand upon the existing law; we feel ourselves to be justified by the law as written. If you think otherwise, we will, in deference to the excellent suggestion made by the British Government to the Paris Congress of 1856, have " recourse to the offices of a friendly power." We will submit the whole matter to arbitration, and abide the result.

But it is said, Mr. Speaker, that the omission to bring in the vessel for adjudication rendered the whole proceeding void *ab initio*. A word upon this point. There is no just ground for complaint of the proceedings, so far as they went. The complaint is, not of what was done, but what was left undone. Two questions arise here: First, was there a sufficient legal reason for not bringing in the vessel? Secondly, what, in the absence of such legal reason, is the effect of the omission?

1. Was there a sufficient reason for not bringing in the "Trent"?

Some things are plain. It is plain that Capt. Wilkes understood that the "Trent" was lawful prize, and that his course was a proceeding in the capture of prize of war. It is plain also that he determined to waive his right to take in the vessel as prize, and to suffer her to proceed on her voyage. These facts are of the highest importance. The difference between the boarding of a vessel by a boat's crew, and taking from her men or goods, — the act constituting no part of a prize proceeding, — and the release of a prize by a captor in the exercise of his discretion, and for reasons of necessity or of humanity, is plain and vital: neither ingenuity nor dulness can confound them. The whole proceedings of Capt. Wilkes were characterized by the utmost good faith. Had he a legal excuse for not bringing in the vessel for adjudication? We do not expect from a sailor, however gallant and accomplished, the precision of special pleading. He gives as the first reason the want of a sufficient prize-crew, in consequence of his being so reduced in officers and men. Was that the fact? It will, I have no doubt, be found to be so. We have now the statement of an officer and a gentleman, and nothing to control it. If such was the fact, and Capt. Wilkes acted upon it, he was justified in law for not bringing the "Trent" in. It is immaterial that motives of humanity concurred with and fortified that conclusion. The heart responded to the head. It neither assumed its prerogative nor questioned it. It only said, "Amen." If the legal excuse existed and was acted upon, it was enough; and the ground upon which the Crown advisers are reported to have proceeded falls from under them.

2. But suppose there was error in not bringing in the vessel: what is the result? It is, that the questions at issue must be settled by the sovereigns of the parties without the aid of a prize-court. The prize-court is the inquest of the sovereign of the captor, and for his protection. It settles the question of seizure, so far as the rights of property are concerned. It does not settle the question of right as between the sovereigns. In this case, the question would have been as to the forfeiture of the vessel: the persons or despatches would not have been directly involved; the judgment would not have operated upon them. If the vessel had been brought in and condemned by a court of admiralty, and England had believed that the judgment of the court was against the law of nations, she would not have acquiesced; she would not have been bound to acquiesce. The same controversy would have opened; the same questions to be settled as now. — *Pinkney's Statement of the Law in the Case of the " Betsey,"* Wheaton's Memoirs of Pinkney, p. 199.

Those questions would have been, Had we the right of search? was it fairly exercised? were the persons taken within the prohibition? and to every one of these questions the law of nations would have answered in the affirmative; and, if England had consulted her oracles, she would have heard the same response. It is not too much to say, that Lord Stowell would have condemned the "Trent" on the double ground of carrying despatches of the enemy and of resistance to search.

Mr. Speaker, when this whole matter shall have been calmly and thoroughly considered and weighed, the judgment of the civilized world will be, or should be, with us. We have the first impression, and not the sober second thought. *The question which has been considered is, rather what the law should be made to be, than what it is.* When the matter is more carefully weighed, it will be seen and felt that no wrong was done to England; that there was no wrong in the forbearance to exercise an extreme right; no insult, for none was intended; that our "failing," if any, "leaned to virtue's side," was a relaxation of the iron rigor of law from motives of humanity and Christian courtesy; that, on the other hand, England has done to us a great wrong in availing herself of our moment of weakness to make a demand, which, accompanied as it was by "the pomp and circumstance of war," was insolent in spirit, unmanly and unjust. It was indeed courteous in language; it was the courtesy of Joab to Amasa as he smote him in the fifth rib: "Art thou in health, my brother?" That message of Lord Russell to Lord Lyons which could cross the Atlantic would not have had projectile force enough to have passed from Dover to Calais.

Such is the penalty of weakness, even temporary weakness.

Upon the grounds upon which this surrender has been made, nothing is gained for the cause of neutral rights.

CASE OF THE TRENT. 99

The lesson taught us by this case is, that not only may every mail steamer of a neutral be seized, and searched for contraband of war or despatches of the enemy, but that her voyage may and must be broken up, and the vessel brought in for adjudication. Neutral commerce may well pray relief from her friends.

But will England feel herself bound by the precedent such as it is? So long as it is convenient, — not a moment longer. Her standard of right has been, is, and will be, the maritime power and interests of England. There is nothing in the " law of nature and of " nations that will stand in the way of her imperious will.

SPEECH AT THE MASS MEETING FOR RECRUITING, ON BOSTON COMMON.

AUGUST 27, 1862.

Mr. PRESIDENT AND FELLOW-CITIZENS,—If you could analyze the feelings of a candle upon being lit up just as the sun was going down, you would appreciate my feelings in succeeding New England's most accomplished orator.* But you neither expect, nor would you tolerate, an elaborate speech. Indeed, if I consulted my own heart, my lips would be sealed.

When the beauty of our Israel is slain on her high places; when the sons of our love are perishing in loathsome dungeons; when armed treason is battering the gates of the capital; when the nation itself is struggling, gasping, for the breath of its life; rhetoric, logic, eloquence even, seem mean and paltry. Nothing, indeed, *is* eloquent but the roar of the cannon and the crack of the rifle, nothing logical but the sword and the bayonet.

The issues before the country are of life or death, glory or shame, order or anarchy, union or chaos, a nation or a Mexico. And, in this hour of awful peril, there is for us but one hope, one way of salvation; and

---
* Mr. Everett.

that is to subdue armed rebellion by arms,—to overwhelm it by superior force on the field of battle.

Processions and banners, touching allusions to Bunker Hill and Faneuil Hall, sentimental resolutions, proclamations beginning and ending in words, bills of confiscation and emancipation, after much travail utterly still born, won't do the work. If you mean to save the country, you have got to fight for it. The negro can't do it for you; Providence won't do it for you, unless you put your shoulders to the wheel. You have got to work out your own salvation; in this case, *without* " fear or trembling."

The only alternative is to sue for peace, and submit to dissolution; to betray the sublime trust committed to us by God and our fathers, and to rot into dishonored graves at home.

If this be so, men of Boston, patriotic, self-sacrificing men, capable of living and dying for your country, what wait you for? The path of duty lies open before you. Interest, duty, honor, patriotism, the sense of manhood, all point one way: that way leads to struggle and to victory, and, through victory, to union and peace. Controversy as to the causes of the war is useless now. Grumbling, carping criticism of the past is mean and disloyal now. Side-issues, partisan or philanthropic, are moral treason now. They weaken and divide us in a struggle that requires all our wisdom, all our energy, all our strength, directed and converged to the single work and duty of subduing the foe in arms. Not a man, not a dollar, not a thought, can be wasted on any other issue. Now or never is the salvation of the country possible. Hard words won't do it; threats and curses won't do it; violence won't do it. Nothing will do it but superior physical force in the field, wielded with an energy all the more terrible because it is calm, and knows how to obey as well as to command.

Fellow-citizens, we have cause for anxiety, — none for despair. We have under-estimated the strength and resources of our opponents. We have greatly under-estimated our own strength and resources. Rebellion has, we may believe, made its crowning effort: its bucket has touched bottom. The water in our well is yet deep. We can maintain a million men in the field; and, on the sea, five hundred ships of war. With these, twenty millions of intelligent, *united*, *devoted* people can vindicate the integrity of the nation, and defy a world in arms.

If you would avoid intervention by foreign powers, the only way is to be prepared for it. Put your million of men into the field, and your five hundred ships upon your seas and rivers. Bear up the old flag, resolved to live under it, to conquer with it, or die beneath its folds. In an hour of your weakness, other nations may intervene; never, if you put forth your real strength, — never.

Would you consent to separation, to give up this glorious Union of your fathers, where will you draw the line? Are the Gulf States only to be severed? Your enemy will not consent to that division. Will you give up the Border States? The Border States will not go. Let me say in the face of the men of Boston, that a nobler, truer, more patriotic set of men, the sun does not shine upon, than the Union men of the Border States. I feel that I know them; and I tell you, they will not go. If finally *driven* from you, no man can say how much of the great West would go with them, or where the ultimate line of division would fall.

[Mr. Thomas here enlarged upon the geographical and commercial ties which bind the West to the South, and said there is no safety for us but in clinging to the Union as it was and the Constitution as it is.]

Let us be manly, be just, be tolerant. It is the easiest thing in the world to find fault, but not the wisest thing. In conducting war upon so vast a scale, and requiring so many and varied agencies, mistakes and blunders will be made. The race is not always to the swift, nor the battle to the strong. We have a great and powerful people, and at their head an upright, conscientious, conservative Chief Magistrate. Let us work, and not grumble; let us labor, and not faint.

THE ARMY OF THE RESERVE.

ADDRESS BEFORE THE PHI BETA KAPPA SOCIETY OF BOWDOIN COLLEGE, AUGUST 7, 1862.

Mr. PRESIDENT AND GENTLEMEN, — Human culture in some one of its aspects is the appropriate theme of the occasion. In selecting the speaker from the field of active and busy life, you did not require nor look for an elaborate discussion of its philosophy. The fair question put to us, wrestlers on the dusty arena, is this: Looking at the subject from your stand-point, have you any practical suggestions to make that may aid us in this noblest of works, — the building-up not only of the living battlements of the State, but of the beings that we are, and are to be?

One of the most important matters in modern warfare is the composition of the army of the reserve. It is relied upon to supply fresh forces at the instant of need, to support points that are shaken, to be ready to act at decisive moments. It should be composed of select troops, well appointed, thoroughly trained, under the eye of a cool, sagacious, and resolute commander. The need of such reserved force has been painfully illustrated in this war for national life. In the most important junctures, we have failed to win victory or secure its fruits from the lack of an army in reserve.

No better example of such a reserve can be found than the Imperial Guard of Napoléon, nor of its use than on the field of Austerlitz.

Our life is a campaign and a warfare. It has its decisive moments, whose issues for good or evil, for victory or defeat, must depend on our reserved power. On the field of letters, on the broader field of human life, he only organizes victory, and commands success, behind whose van and corps of battle is heard the steady tramp of the army of the reserve.

To some illustrations of this thought I give the hour your kindness has assigned to me.

It is a stern lesson, and hard to be learned, that though the ordinary duties of life require large power, intellectual and moral, the supply must constantly exceed the immediate demand. It is a hard lesson, but a necessary one.

Life is not all routine. It has its great temptations, its golden opportunities. To withstand the one, to seize the other, we must organize and maintain our spiritual army of the reserve. There is no hope of large achievement, or of safety even, in impressing forces or foraging for supplies on the line of march, much less on the eve of battle. In youth for manhood, in summer for winter, in sunshine for storm, in peace for war, in the actual for the possible, the law of Providence and foresight is universal.

The rules for the composition of the spiritual reserve are simple, whatever of difficulty there may be in their just application. Faculties trained by patient, thorough, protracted discipline; supplies carefully garnered, and then so thoroughly digested that they will enter into the bone and muscle of the mind, and become power; this was what Lord Bacon meant by saying knowledge was power.

The nucleus is to be formed before the campaign of active life opens; after that, growing rigor of discipline and daily accessions of strength.

The magnitude and extent of the reserve are to be measured, not by the wants of to-day or of the next campaign, but by the possible exigencies of human life, — a life whose horizon is ever lifting up, whose possibilities of to-day are the necessities of to-morrow.

And though there must be limitation, and exclusion even, no more forces than can be well kept up and maintained, no half-grown conscripts, none maimed or blind, diseased or leprous, yet the recruiting-office is never closed; for the campaign is never ended.

We have thrift and providence; but they take a material direction. We save for the dark and rainy day; but we save money and houses and lands. Intellectually, we live from hand to mouth. We begin the life of action before the life of study. The result is, that, with most of us, the life of patient study and quiet thought *never* begins. " Quid enim aut didicimus aut scire potuimus qui ante ad agendum quam ad cognescendum venimus."

Getting knowledge for immediate use, cramming for the occasion, we limit ourselves to the narrowest range of the useful and practical: meaning, by *useful*, value in the shambles of the market; and by *practical*, dexterity in the use of tools, without any perception of the principles which underlie them. We find, often too late except as a warning to others, that there is nothing in this world half so practical or half so economical as accurate knowledge, patient labor, thorough discipline, the careful composition, the constant training, of the army of the reserve.

And first we may remark, that this reserved power is necessary to the thorough possession of ourselves. It is true, abstractly, that a man owns himself, his powers and faculties; but, in ninety-nine cases in an hundred, he never comes into the quiet enjoyment of his estate. With some opportunities for observing men in intellectual conflict, I venture to say there is no respect in which the difference is so marked as in the extent to which they possess themselves, their own powers and resources. We hear much of self-culture and self-development; and it is well. All true culture is self-culture; all true development is self-development. We hear far less than we ought of the thorough possession of a man's self; of spiritual forces so orderly disposed, so loyal, so trained to prompt obedience and action, that they will rally, and form into line for service, at the first tap of the drum.

There are men, with all the learning of the schools, whose learning is but a clog and hinderance: their learning masters them, not they their learning; creating such a pressure on the brain, that it has no free, natural play and motion; ever coming in at the wrong time, or coming in too late; like the baggage of an eastern army, the great impediment to the march; or rather like the undisciplined hordes of nations that followed Xerxes from Asia to the plains of Doriscus, and from Doriscus to

Thermopylæ. Better, infinitely better, one well-trained Spartan band.

Necessary to this self-possession are calmness, — the calmness which springs only from the consciousness of strength in reserve, of measured strength, of power to strike the needed blow at the decisive moment; the orderly disposition of our forces, a place for every thing, and every thing in its place; the military eye which surveys the whole field of action, sees where the fight will be thickest and hardest, and the forces needed; and, rarest of powers, the power to refrain, to withhold your fire; to sit still when there is no occasion to be on your feet; the power and gift of silence, the power to say nothing when you have nothing to say, or nothing that had not better be unsaid; the power of masterly inactivity, the effective grace of repose.

Instead of schools to teach us how to talk, we want schools to teach us how to be silent; sanitary clubs and commissions, whose end and aim shall be to prevent the spread of this *insanabile cacoethes loquendi*.

In this power of self-mastery is wrapped the faculty and grace and liberty of obedience; the power to recognize the presence of law, and to bend to it; to mark its bounds, and keep within them. " Qui nescit ignorare ignorat scire." The rebellious is never the truly wise spirit. It is for ever breaking and bruising itself against the walls of its fancied prison-house. Into the obedient, ever open, and receptive spirit, wisdom loves to come and take up her abode.

He only well commands who knows to serve well, to obey promptly, gracefully, with thorough loyalty of mind d heart; the rarest of virtues, not the peculiar virtue of our countrymen, very apt to confound the absence of wholesome restraint with liberty; whereas true freedom is for the loyal soul, — liberty in law. The loyal spirit feels restraint as a woman wears the bracelet on her white arm; the rebel spirit, as the culprit the handcuffs on his galled and swollen wrists.

Again: we remark, that the gathering and training of this army of the reserve is the easiest and cheapest way of conducting, not a great war only, but the campaign of life.

If a man means to do any thing in this world to win the battle of life, it is easier to *be* than to *seem*. In the long-run, reality is easier than sham, wisdom than cunning, the king's highway than the by-path or cross-cut. It is often a simpler thing to acquire strength than to conceal the lack of it. Nothing indeed is more exhausting than the shifts to cover up ignorance; the craft required to seem to know what a man knows not; the constant caution, lest our hollow wares should come to the light; the everlasting repetition " of wise saws and modern instances;" the perpetual dread of being found out, — that the blown bladder may be pierced by some shaft of ridicule, and collapse for ever; to say nothing of the sinking of the knees, the drooping of the head, and the suffusion of blood upon the brain.

"The easiest way," said Sir Boyle Roche, " to avoid danger, is to meet it plump. If there is work in a man's way, the best possible thing that can be done is to go through it, and on a man's own feet. If he ride round it, nine chances out of ten he must come back, and walk straight through it." It often costs less labor to do work than to avoid it. Looking at a specific work or duty, the simplest and best thing is to do it, and do it well if you can. Looking at life as a whole, the truth of the remark becomes yet clearer. The doing of a thing well not only prevents the necessity of doing it again, but adds to the mind's reserved force, and renders the doing of the next thing easier and simpler. The resisting of one temptation helps to disarm the power of the second. It is not long before labor and self-denial become positive enjoyments, and this without including the *gaudia certaminis*, or the highest of all possible satisfactions, the purest of all possible delights, — the consciousness of duty discharged.

There can be no real comfort or satisfaction in a campaign in which you have to rely upon raw, undisciplined, not to say mutinous forces, hastily conscripted, acting without system or concert. You must feel there is a reserved force, well appointed and trained, upon which you can draw in a moment of need; whose strength you have measured; and which, great or small, is reliable and forthcoming.

For example: A young man is to study law. It is his business to understand it, and expound it to others. Fidelity to his clients and to his oath of office requires this. He cannot, with decent self-respect or as an honest man, assume to say what the law is, unless he has diligently sought to know what it is. The best, the cheapest thing he can do for his campaign of life, is to bring to the study of the law a mind well trained and enriched by liberal culture, and then to set about the mastery of its principles. This training, this culture, this mastery of principles, will make up a glorious army of the reserve, the worth of which, his life long, can never be overrated; the want of which, his life long, can never be supplied. Men of genius and untiring industry have, indeed, a measure of success without them. But they, of all men, most deeply regret their lack; for they, of all men, best understand what larger victories might have been gracefully won with their aid.

How common, on the other hand, utter failure from the want of this reserved power!

A young man of fair powers, but of little or no training, is anxious, restless, for active life. He would enter upon the arena not only unarmed, but incapable of bearing the weight of armor. He will have only practical knowledge. When the occasion comes, he will study for it. He has what are called *promising* qualities; qualities which seldom or never *pay*. He has a certain facility of acquisition, but retains nothing save the confidence which such facility is apt to beget. He talks fluently, never hesitates for a word, and seldom gets the right one. He writes with perfect ease, and therefore never writes well. He never doubts, and therefore never understands.

His wished-for opportunity comes. He gets up a great array of cheap learning and cheaper eloquence; enters upon the contest with drum beating and banner flying. Difficulties spring up he had not foreseen, and he has no reserved force to meet them. He shrivels, and his client's cause with him. The way of life is strewn with sprouts like this. "Having no root in themselves, they endure but for a time."

It is obvious to remark, that, in life as in war, the force which may suffice for ordinary service may be wholly inadequate for its larger exigencies, for its decisive moments. In almost every life, those decisive moments come, when the question of victory or defeat, of pressing onward or lingering behind, must depend upon our reserved power; when the door of opportunity is swung open, and, if ready, we may enter; if not, the door closes upon us.

Great occasions do not *make* great men. (Of this the country needs no proof.) They find them out, and give them larger development and a broader theatre of action. Great men *make* great occasions. They impart to them a strength, a beauty, a glory of their own. They bathe and irradiate them with the light of their genius. They give to them of their own immortality. Nay, more: great men *are* great occasions, the great events of history; not merely the beacon-lights on the line of human progress, but the efficient motive-powers, the *causæ causantes*: they make, they constitute history. Their hands bend the arch of the new heaven, and mould the new earth, if so be that they feel the Divine Arm around them and upholding them, and do the work of God with the armor of God. I have no great faith in "village Hampdens" or the "mute, inglorious Miltons" that rest in country churchyards. If a man has a lever to move the world, the chances are that he will find a place to put it. Genius is very apt to crop out: so men of large reserved power are apt to find occasions to bring it into action, to give it effective utterance.

THE ARMY OF THE RESERVE.   113

The introduction, into the Senate of the United States, of a resolution in relation to the sale of the public lands, was not a great occasion. The debate upon it for some days dragged heavily. The vast reserved power of one man made it the event of our history for a generation.

The second speech of Mr. Hayne, to which Mr. Webster was called upon to reply, was able and brilliant, its constitutional argument specious, its attack upon New England and upon Mr. Webster sharp even to bitterness. But Mr. Hayne did *not* understand this matter of reserved power. He had seen Mr. Webster's van and corps of battle, but had not heard the firm and measured tread behind.

It was a decisive moment in Mr. Webster's career. He had no time to impress new forces; scarcely time to burnish his armor. All eyes were turned to him. Some of his best friends were depressed and anxious. *He* was calm as a summer's morning; calm, his friends thought, even to indifference. But his calmness was the repose of conscious power, the hush of nature before the storm. He had measured his strength. He was in possession of himself. He knew the composition of his "army of the reserve." He had the eye of a great commander, and he took in the whole field at a glance. He had the prophetic eye of logic, and he saw the end from the beginning. The exordium itself was the prophecy, the assurance, of victory. Men saw the sun of Austerlitz, and felt that the Imperial Guard was moving on to the conflict. He came out of the conflict with the immortal name of the Defender of the Constitution.

Of this speech, and the mode of its delivery, one of the greatest of our orators has said, " It has been my fortune to hear some of the ablest speeches of the greatest living orators on both sides of the water; but I must confess, I never heard any thing which so completely realized my conception of what Demosthenes was when he delivered the Oration for the Crown." I venture to add, that, taking into view the circumstances under which the speech was delivered, especially the brief time for preparation, the importance of the subject, the breadth of its views, the strength and clearness of its reasoning, the force and beauty of its style, its keen wit, its repressed but subduing passion, its lofty strains of eloquence, the audience to which it was addressed (a more than Roman Senate), its effect upon that audience, and the larger audience of a grateful and admiring country, history has no nobler example of reserved power brought at once and effectively into action. The wretched sophistries of nullification and secession were swept before his burning eloquence as the dry grass is swept by the fire of the prairies.

The general impression in hearing Mr. Webster was, I think, that, great as was the speech, the man was greater than the speech; that there was vast reserved power behind the power in action. Sometimes it was brought to the conflict at a moment's warning. I remember such an occasion some fourteen years ago. It was at a small assembly of about an hundred gentlemen. Mr. Webster had spoken, in reply to a sentiment in his honor, well, but without great life or vigor. A remark by a subsequent speaker looked like a reflection upon his public course. It were better to have roused the lion from his lair. There was no sudden spring, no visible passion; but you could see and feel that the very depths of his being were stirred. Those dark eyes, in their deep, dark caverns, glowed like stars. The hall in which we sat vibrated with the vibrations of his thought.

The speech I will not assume to report. One of the topics, I remember, was his relations with the Commonwealth of Massachusetts, the open arms with which she had received him, the kindness she had heaped upon him, the trust and confidence she had reposed in him. His great heart became liquid as he spoke, and he poured it out in love, loyalty, and gratitude: then, drawing himself up to his full stature, till through our moist and loving eyes his proportions seemed colossal, he said, with quiet dignity but with trembling lips, "I have dared to hope, Mr. President and gentlemen, that I have not proved myself wholly unworthy of her trust and confidence." I never before understood the lines of Milton: —

> "The angel ended, but in Adam's ear
> So charming left his voice, that he awhile
> Thought him still speaking, still stood fixed to hear."

He sleeps well by the sea he loved so well.

His prayer was granted. When his eyes were turned to behold for the last time the sun in heaven, he did not see him shining on the broken and dishonored fragments of a once-glorious Union.

There is another reason for the composition and discipline of the army of the reserve, to which I attach much importance. It is, that power in reserve is necessary to give full force and effect to power in action. Of the impressions made upon us by the use of great power, material or spiritual, one of the most striking, I think, is the sense it creates of power not used; of power behind the power in action, greater than itself. The power which is wholly spent and exhausted in the effort loses half its charm. For its highest effect, it must beget the impression, that we see but in part, the arc of a power full-orbed, the stream from a full, overflowing fountain, the vanguard of a greater host. We do not admire the well whose bottom is hit by every dip of the bucket, the mill-pond that is drained for one grist (even if it be *our* corn), the picture without a background, the quiver with one arrow, the hen with one chicken, the mind with one idea, the heavens with one star, even if it be the north star.

A speech seems to us truly great, only when a man stands behind it who is greater than the speech, with power in reserve; not if it plainly drains his memory, exhausts his vocabulary, and stretches his brain to lesion. It is not merely what is said, but who says it; not merely what he says, but what he is.

When, in a crisis of our history, there was given, at a festive celebration in Washington, the sentiment, " The Federal Union, it *must* be *preserved*," the words and the thought were familiar and commonplace; but the devoted patriotism, the energetic brain, the commanding spirit, the unflinching courage, the iron will, of Andrew Jackson were behind the words, and the country breathed more freely for their utterance. Would to God our heroes were not all in history!

THE ARMY OF THE RESERVE. 117

> "Clan-Alpine's best are backward borne:
> Where, where, was Roderick then?
> One blast upon his bugle-horn
> Were worth a thousand men."

Of material power, it is also true, that its effect is deepened and strengthened by the sense of a greater power behind the power we see or hear or feel.

Night, solemn, glorious night, with its hosts of stars, has its army of the reserve, of suns and stars behind the stars we see, in infinite procession; the countless legions whose banners of light never yet waved to mortal eye.

Nature indeed, in her beauty or in her grandeur; in the dewdrop sparkling in the chalice of a flower, or in Mont Blanc touched with the first light of morning; in the field-brook that sings with the singing corn, or in Erie pouring out its world of waters; in summer's breeze or winter's tempest; in glassy lake or surging ocean; first deeply impresses us when we feel its reserved power, see on its face the smile, and read in its living lines the thoughts, of God.

Art also touches and moves us by its reserved power.

This picture is true to the rules, the idea of the painter fairly brought out, the work finished even with the minutest detail of Dusseldorf. It is not without power, but power fully spent and exhausted. We look and comprehend it, and do not care to look again. It has no reserved power; nothing to pay for a second coming.

Here is another, of which a critic has said, "It was a crude painted medley, with a general foggy appearance." Be not dismayed; look again, look into it. The fog gradually lifts up, and the picture comes out of seeming chaos, and marshals itself into light and order and beauty. Some mist may yet hang over it; but it glows and is alive with the genius and the inspiration of the poet-painter.

In the great masters of English thought (of the *world's* thought), you have striking examples of this reserved power. You read an Essay of Bacon, or the "Advancement of Learning," twenty times. New forces of wisdom and beauty come out at every reading. You find the most diligent study has not exhausted the depths of meaning. With a telescopic vision, what seem to be nebulæ now would be resolved into burning stars. You get some idea of the height and breadth of Bacon by reading the edition of his Essays by Whately. The archbishop is a sensible man, of large mental stature; but how he looks trotting along by the side of Lord Bacon, and occasionally throwing over his shoulders a corner of the giant's mantle!

And the great master of the drama; the priest who sat at the confessional of the human passions; the philosopher who unravelled the mysteries of our being as the cunning fingers of Miss Prissy would untangle a snarled thread; the child of Nature, who laid his ear so close to his mother's heart that he could hear its faintest beatings; historian, statesman, sage, poet (ΠΟΙΗΤΕΣ, *maker*): such is our sense of reserved power in him, that what we most admire and love, as " Hamlet," " Macbeth," " Lear," the " Tempest," seem really but the *plays* of Shakspeare, the *sport* and *pastime* of his mighty spirit; waves born to our feet from a deep sea our oar has never vexed or plummet sounded.

Burke, whom the late Mr. Buckle would put in a strait-jacket, but who will be likely to outlive his keepers; (*quis custodiet custodes?*) whose volume of thought pours out very much as Niagara pours over the Horseshoe, with the rapid's thunder, the mist, the spray, the bow of everlasting beauty; never seems exhausted, but as if there were an hundred inland seas of thought behind, waiting to be poured out.

A little reflection will satisfy us how constantly, though it may be unconsciously, we use this test of the fulness or want of reserved power. You read a book, an essay, or an article in a review, and you determine almost at a glance whether the matter has just been pumped into the author's skull, and then pumped out again, or whether he draws from a full living spring. The modern multiplication of books is, for the most part, the pouring of water from one pitcher into another. Very few of them are mixed, as Mr. Opie mixed his colors, with brains. As we grow older, we seek the fountains, the old wells of English undefiled; for the great teachers of the race and of the coming generations have spoken or written in our mother-tongue. I shall go to my grave, I fear, in the delusion that Bacon,

"In one rich soul,
Plato, the Stagyrite, and Tully, joined;"

that Shakspeare held the perfect mirror up to nature; that the "Paradise Lost" is the greatest of epics, if not the first; that, of written and forensic eloquence, the great masters are Edmund Burke and Thomas Erskine; that no man is fitted for the bar, the pulpit, or the chair of instruction, who has not given himself to the diligent and thorough study of the English classics. A certain grace, polish, refinement, may be got in other schools: these constitute our *pabulum vitæ*.

Reserved power may not always prevent partial defeat or temporary failure; but it will avert the dismay and despondency which too often follow partial failure. The man of reserved power may bend before the storm; but he will bend only as, Landor says, " the oak bends before the passing wind, to rise again in its majesty and in its strength." Nay, it seems at times as if, Antæus-like, he got new strength from contact with the earth, new vigor from the fall. Apparent defeat may be real victory; the moving from Moultrie to Sumter. His army of the reserve may not have been brought into action at the needed moment. He will be ready for another trial. He knows the power is in him, and will do its work.

We all remember the case of Sheridan. After his first speech in the House of Commons, he asked Mr. Woodfall what he thought of it. "I am sorry to say, I do not think it is in your line. You had much better have stuck to your old pursuits." — "It is *in* me, and it shall come *out*." It did indeed come out. He lived to hear from Pitt (no longer sneering Pitt) the motion, that the House of Commons should adjourn to recover from the effects of Mr. Sheridan's eloquence.

The brilliant writer and statesman D'Israeli, late Chancellor of the Exchequer, and leader of the House of Commons, was literally groaned and sneered down in his first attempt to speak upon the floor. He knew his reserved strength. " The day will come when you will be glad to hear me." It came long ago. He is to-day, with the exception of his successor, Mr. Gladstone, the most effective debater in the Commons of England.

The material army of the reserve, though trained by the discipline of conflict and endurance, is worn and wasted by the same cause. Its thinned and broken ranks must be filled and replenished with new life, new brain, bone, and muscle.

It is not wholly so with the spiritual army of the reserve. This, too, is trained and strengthened by struggle and suffering; but, in this, every accretion of power is permanent; every enlistment not only for the campaign of life, but for the life everlasting. It is a beautiful doctrine, which the study of the human mind tends more and more to confirm, that knowledge, once gained, is never lost; that we never really forget; that what we call imperfection of memory is but a defect in the material instrument, some mist or dulness in the mirror which reflects the beam of light. It is a beautiful doctrine, but a fearful one; suggesting the questions, What knowledges have we garnered in this everlasting storehouse? on what spiritual breads have we fed, that have thus entered into the very substance and framework of our being? what unfading pictures have been frescoed on the ever-enduring walls of the soul?

It is, I trust, scarcely necessary to suggest, that though our spiritual powers enlarge by use, and are nurtured by effort and struggle, there are limits to the law; that they do not grow by over-work; that the bow must not always be bent, and never strained. I have no faith in working with jaded powers, or in holding up, as exemplars to the young, the men who give their nights as well as days to study.

> "And wherefore does the student trim his lamp,
> And watch his lonely taper, when the stars
> Are holding their high festival in heaven,
> And worshipping around the midnight throne?"

The just and sensible answer to this glowing question is, Because he don't know any better; because he don't understand, or care to recognize and obey, the laws of his spiritual as well as physical health and life. It were far better for him to be infolded in the arms of "Nature's sweet restorer, gentle sleep."

In a busy life, we cannot measure our daily work by exact rules. The true rule is, to work much, not many hours. More work must be done on one day than another: but eight hours of mental labor is enough for the most vigorous constitution; more than most men can do with safety. He who seeks to do more must often bring to his work a flagging brain; or if he be of the class, who, when they work, must work with intensity, break, not indeed his spirit vital in every part, but the material instruments by which it works.

No better illustration of these truths can be found than in New England's most accomplished advocate.

Of brilliant powers, enriched by wide and varied culture; of rapid perceptions; of retentive and capacious memory; of rich, glowing, Oriental imagination; of a quiet and subtle wit, whose delicate aroma it is in vain to hope to preserve; with that projectile force of mind which is the peculiar trait of a great advocate; with a logic keen and vigorous, though, like the dagger of Harmodius, it was often hidden beneath the myrtles; with a heart gentle as a woman's, yet capable of stiffening its sinews; with little inclination to social life, yet the most delightful of companions, — Mr. Choate was, at the bar or in his own library, the most interesting man it has been my privilege to know: yet, during the last six years of his life (and it was during those years I saw him most frequently), I never heard him, even in the most brilliant of his efforts, without a feeling of sadness. He not only worked too much, but he had no just economy of labor. He did a thousand things which men of narrower capacity might have done as well, or well enough. He expended upon his work a vast amount of superfluous strength. He brought the whole army of the reserve into action, when the victory might have been easily and gracefully won by the van and corps of battle. If he had tried half as many causes, worked half as many hours, he would have been a yet greater man, and his life might have been spared to the courts of which he was the pride and ornament; nay, more, those large and generous powers might have been used upon a broader theatre, and for nobler and more enduring service. As it was, we may write upon his monument the inscription upon the bust of Erskine at Holland House: —

"Nostræ eloquentiæ forensis facile princeps."

Pardon one or two practical suggestions.

We all need this reserved power; but it comes only from the union of contemplation and action. Our life is stir, bustle, everlasting motion; the whistle of the engine, the click of the telegraph.

> "We pry not into the interior; but, like the martlet,
> Build in the weather, on the outward wall,
> Even in the force and road of casualty."

The business of life should be so conducted as to give us time for quiet study and meditation. The best processes of culture must be perfected in our own libraries, with patient toil and thought.

The mind requires not only diversity of discipline, but generosity of diet. It will not grow to full, well-rounded proportions and robust strength upon any one aliment.

There is no profession or pursuit in life, which, followed with exclusive devotion, will not narrow and contract the mind.

Philanthropy is a good thing; but, if a man lives upon it, it sours the milk, and curdles the blood, till the love of the race becomes the hatred of every man and woman that compose it.

Theology is a good thing; but, if a man fed upon that only, his bones would cleave to his skin. The teacher of it must, by constant reading and study, replenish the exhausted fountains of thought. It is the spider only that weaves from his own entrails, and he weaves in circles. The writer without such refreshment is the constant repetition of himself; the turning of the wheel upon its own axis; incessant motion, but no progress; the travelling in the same old ruts with the old " one-hoss shay."

The law is a good thing; but no man can be a great lawyer who knows nothing else. The study and practice of the law tend to acumen rather than breadth, to subtlety rather than strength. The air is thin among the apices of the law, as on the granite needles of the Alps. We must come down for refreshment and strength to the quiet valleys at their feet.

Pope was wrong. The Ovid was not in Murray lost. Lord Mansfield was the greater lawyer and judge, because the Ovid grew and was developed in him. For his comprehensive grasp of great principles, for those large constructive powers by which he built up the modern commercial law of England, for the beauty and crystal clearness of his style, we are indebted, in no small degree, to his wide and varied culture.

The law is *not* a " jealous mistress: " she is a very sensible mistress. She does not object to an evening with the Muses or the Graces, provided we do not remain into the small hours of the morning. The farewell of Blackstone to his Muse is unnecessarily pathetic. The confused air and shuffling gait with which he takes his leave of her ladyship indicate that the relations were not very intimate or confidential. He was in no danger.

Commerce is a noble thing. The pioneer of civilization, the diplomatist of peace, " her line is gone out through all the earth, and her words to the end of the world." But a man cannot live upon the bread of traffic only. He needs a yet higher commerce (to modify the thought of Bacon); the unfreighting of those ships that come down to us through the vast seas of time, laden with the wisdom of ages.

The country must have its reserved power. It consists, not in wider dominion, in material progress, in wealth, in luxury, in the subjection of nature to the mind and will of man. These but enlarge the theatre of human passions and interests: the actors and the drama remain the same.

Have we no reason to fear, that, in subduing the earth, the earth has, to some extent, subdued us; that, while mind has mastered matter, it has also worshipped it; that we have given our hearts to the idols which our cunning fingers have moulded; that ours has become the condition of Faust, when he summoned to his presence the spirit of the earth, and felt, at first, his energies exalted and glowing as with new wine, but found he could not mate himself with the spirit he had evoked, and, in his despair, exclaimed, "If I had the power to draw thee to me, I have no power to hold thee"?

Our strength, our reserved power, is in our fidelity to the principles on which these States were founded, in which their youth was nurtured, by which they were ripened together into one national life; loyalty to freedom, obedience to law, then, now, and for ever, one and inseparable.

The founders of the Republic did not believe that government was merely moral suasion; that liberty was the absence of wholesome restraint; that laws were to be obeyed only when obedience was agreeable; the country to be defended and saved only when the subject should volunteer; that the Constitution was to be supreme only when it was convenient; the Union a mere silken string, from which States might be slipped by secession or severed by treason. No enduring fabric can rest on such dogmas. The roots of civil government strike deep, and find nutriment and support in the depths of the Divine Will. Law is a sword as well as a shield; there is no liberty but within its pale: the defence of the country, at the cost of treasure or of life, is the first of civil duties; the Constitution, in war as in peace, is the supreme law, the bond of equal States, inseparable, without limit of time, immutable except in the mode itself points out.

These plain principles, now somewhat old-fashioned, not to say obsolete, make up for the country its moral army of the reserve.

Brethren, this dear country of ours is in extreme peril For her succor and deliverance, she needs all your wisdom and all your strength, the counsels of age, the vigor of manhood, the flower of youth. God of our fathers, gird us for the work: by tribulation and suffering, by this baptism of fire and of blood, purify and gird us for the work of her salvation. God of our fathers, we can save her, and we will. Redeemed, purified, plucked as a brand from the burning, we will give her once more to thy service, in which alone is perfect freedom.

SPEECH AT CHELSEA.

October 31, 1862.

Fellow-Citizens, — An important election is at hand. No thoughtful man ever casts a vote without inquiry as to his duty. At a time like this, he is painfully anxious. He feels he cannot use it to gratify personal or party predilections; that it belongs to the country, and must be so given as best to serve her interests. For eighteen months we had been engaged in a civil war, whose extent, whose intense bitterness, whose consumption of treasure and of most precious blood, have no parallel in history. The struggle was tasking to the uttermost the resources of the loyal States. The people believed the war was just and necessary. They saw no hope for the country but in its vigorous prosecution. They had been grievously disappointed by the want of progress in suppressing the Rebellion. They were mortified and chagrined by disasters and defeats, followed by lame and impotent apologies. They were disgusted by the frauds of contractors, the jealousies of commanders, the selfishness of politicians, the want of unity, method, and persistent vigor in the public counsels, with the presence everywhere of politicians and office-holders, unchastened by the public calamities, obtruding upon the Executive councils, dictating to Congress, meddling with the command and direction of the armies, seeking to control the elections, growing fat upon the public distresses. Many of them were grieved and alarmed at the absence of respect, to use no harsh word, manifested by some of their servants for the ancient and sacred muniments of personal liberty; without which, free government is a mockery, and life itself a burden. Hope deferred was making the heart sick. In that day of distraction and anxiety and thick gloom, one thing seemed to be as clear as the sun at mid-day; and that was, the necessity of an united North; that all its wisdom, all its energy, all its strength, should be combined, converged, projected into one purpose, one issue, one aim, — the suppression of armed rebellion by force of arms.

As this was a common cause, infinitely transcending all party questions, with which Republican, Whig, and Democrat were alike concerned; for which, justice compels us to say, they had made equal sacrifices, and must share equal burdens; *as the peculiar objects for which the party in power had been organized were already attained by the legislation of Congress;* no sound, substantial reason existed for upholding the old party barriers, or drawing, with any rigor, the old party lines. On the other hand, patriotism and sound policy seemed to require that party organizations should, during the war at least, be given up; for these organizations, though often the *result* of differences of opinion, are as often the *cause*. When men are working together for a common end, and with no visible line of separation, they will converge, assimilate, and cleave together. Make a breach between them which is palpable, and, however narrow at first, it will constantly widen. Differences, slight at the start, will enlarge by conflict and repulsion, till unity of action and effort are no longer practicable.

The Republican party has had, and has now, the ascendency in this Commonwealth. It was inclined at first to pursue a liberal policy. It would to-day, if its wise and prudent men controlled its movements. It is made up of two wings. The first consists of those who are opposed to slavery; who desire to see its restriction within its present limits, and its removal from places where the power of the National Government is supreme; but who also hold, "that the maintenance inviolate of the rights of the States, and especially the right of each State to order and control its own domestic institutions according to its own judgment exclusively, is essential to that balance of powers on which the perfection and endurance of our political fabric depends" (Chicago Platform); and that the war is prosecuted "for the purpose of practically restoring the constitutional relations between the United States and each of the States and the people thereof, in which States that relation is or may be suspended or disturbed" (President's Proclamation of Sept. 22); and that, when this object is attained, the war ought to cease. This is the Conservative wing.

The other wing consists of those, who, for want of a better word, may be called Abolitionists; men who, with more or less indirection, circuitous navigation of thought and word, come at last to the point, that Constitution or no Constitution, Union or no Union, endure the war as long as it may, be the cost and carnage and exhaustion what they may, slavery shall be abolished. This wing of the party is now in the ascendant, and rules the party with a rod of iron. They arranged and controlled the Annual Convention. They saw to it that no man was nominated who did not embrace their extreme views, though they were kind enough to include some very recent converts. They covered their leaders with adulation thicker than a man's loins, and snubbed the President of the United States because their platform was too narrow for him to stand upon. They made the test of loyalty, fidelity to men, instead of devotion to the country. This wing of the party arranges and controls all the preliminary meetings, sets in motion all the party machinery, and makes all the party nominations. So far as its power extends, not a man, holding what are usually termed conservative views, will be elected to any place, state or national. Never was proscription so rigid, so bitter, so universal. They go now one step further. Assuming that the President has at last yielded to their pressure, and has adopted their policy, they denounce as a traitor every man who hesitates as to the wisdom of the proclamation, or who fails to give it their interpretation. Without stopping to murmur or complain, one may be permitted to say, that such charges come with little grace from men, who, but a few weeks ago, felt the defence of the country, under the then policy, to be a heavy draft upon their patriotism; with still less grace from those of them who have for years been laboring to destroy the blessed Union of our fathers, and who even now repudiate it with hissing and scorn.

In this condition of things, the severance of political associations is natural, is perhaps inevitable. The differences of principle and of policy are too great to be reconciled. The Radicals, upon their own showing, neither want nor need our aid. We, the Conservatives, must be true to our convictions of duty, and stand to the last by the Union and Constitution. But, while these differences of opinion and policy exist, we can unite in the vigorous prosecution of this war till the rebels lay down their arms, whoever shall constitute the National and State administrations. *We can give them a vigorous and unhesitating support in the discharge of this great and imperative duty.* We can and should avoid all captious opposition or criticism; but we may not and will not surrender our judgments or our consciences. We will not forget who are the servants, and who the masters. We will elect, if we can, to places of power, men who reflect our opinions. We will send men to Congress who will sustain the Administration in all constitutional and just measures, and hold them back, if possible, from a radical and destructive policy. We don't propose to rehabilitate the doctrine of passive obedience, or of an infallible political church. *In war, as in peace, freedom of thought and utterance is to the body politic what vital air is to the human system. It cannot live without it.*

I am one of those who are content with the Constitution as it is, and the Union as it was; the Constitution fairly interpreted in the spirit of its founders. I have felt no misgivings, and had no mental reservations, in swearing to support it. To me the oath was the pledge, not of duty merely, but of love and devotion. I mean to keep that oath; and, with such strength as may be given me, to uphold and defend that Constitution, because the life of the nation is bound up in it; because the preservation of the Constitution, and the preservation of the Union, are not *two* questions, but *one* question; are not *two* issues, but *one and the same issue*. I have lived half a century without discovering or suspecting that the "Constitution was a failure." On the other hand, I have ever regarded it as the noblest product of the human mind; the work of men chastened by adversity, disciplined by trial; in their conscious weakness, seeking the Divine Strength; believing that God governs in the affairs of men; assured that, "except the Lord build the house, they labor in vain who build it." That Constitution has given us a Government felt only in its blessings; under whose benign and quickening influences the nation sprung up to greatness, her commerce whitening every sea, the stars on her banner kindled by the light of a never-setting sun; a model Republic, which won for itself the homage and admiration of mankind, — the fear of kings, to struggling humanity, inspiration and hope. It is very easy to say the Constitution is not perfect. I am not wise enough to build a better, and do not know the men who are. It is easy to express regret at what are called its compromises. You may as well regret it was ever made. All government is compromise, save as it is rooted in the Divine Will. Social order is mutual concession. The Constitution was the best compromise that could be made; and the experience of more than seventy years has not taught us how to make a wiser one.

That Constitution is the bond of national unity. Rebellion, under the guise of Secession, sought to sever the bond, to cut the thread of the national life. We grasped the sword to vindicate the Constitution, to save the national unity. Never was the sword drawn in a holier cause. Never was a war *more just or more strictly defensive.* It was not only the sacred right and duty of government to wage it, but the necessity of its being. *That right, in its length and its breadth, is the right to enforce the laws. Within the pale of the Constitution, States and people may be held to obedience. Outside of that pale, the whole struggle is revolutionary.* I put the plain question to every honest conscience, How can I, by force of arms, by fire, and the sword, compel obedience to a law I do not respect myself? How can I vindicate the law with the sword in my right hand, and break it with the hammer in my left? No subtlety of logic, no refinement of casuistry, can evade or conceal the answer. The right of revolution remains intact; but this Government has never pretended that it was waging a war of revolution. Its claim, thus far, has been to wage a war *under* the Constitution *for* the Constitution. This plain view of the struggle I have taken from the beginning. The progress of events has served to deepen my conviction of its soundness. I never doubted that the Constitution clothed the Government with all powers necessary to the efficient prosecution of the war. I never doubted that fidelity to that Constitution was our safety and strength, and that every way that diverged from it was the way to death.

The common mode of argument is to assume that a certain policy is necessary, and then to infer that it is within the Constitution. Take, for example, the policy of confiscating the property of non-combatants, outside of the conflict of arms, and without conviction of the owner. The measure is, in my judgment, in direct conflict with the Constitution; but it is also in conflict with the law of nations, and with every principle of justice and humanity. The judgment and conscience of every Christian nation condemn it. Such a law is not a source of strength, but of weakness. With all deference to the judgment of others, I feel it my duty to say, that the unconstitutional measures passed or proposed by the Radical party in Congress have done as much to protract the war as all the treasure that has been spent, and all the blood that has been shed, have done to end it. They shook the public faith and confidence. Men cannot be taught to understand, that, in enforcing the law, it is necessary to break it; or, in upholding the Constitution, it is necessary to violate it. These measures weakened our cause in the Border States, which every practical man has seen, from the beginning, to be the battle-ground of this contest; retaining which, our ultimate triumph was almost certain; losing which, there was no solid ground of hope for the Union. The policy, moreover, cost us the few friends we had in the rebel States. It kindled into greater intensity the hatred of the foe, and nerved him to a yet more desperate and bitter struggle. It divided the public sentiment of the North, and wounded the Government in the house of its friends. My policy in this struggle is the vigorous prosecution of the war, with careful adherence to the Constitution, and the maxims of moderation and humanity with which civilization and

Christianity have tempered the ancient iron rules of war. Whenever decisive victories are achieved, I would issue a general proclamation of amnesty and pardon, excepting only a few of the leaders most deeply steeped in guilt. Under all circumstances, I would cling to the Constitution, as the bond of unity in the past, as the only practical bond of Union in the future; the only land lifted above the waters on which the ark of Union can be moored. From that ark alone will go out the Dove blessed of the Spirit, which shall return bringing in its mouth the olive branch of peace.

The policy of the Abolitionists is expressed in the phrase, the Union as it should be, or the Union without slavery. No policy could be more attractive. But let us probe the words, and get at the depth of their meaning. An Union without slavery implies not merely that the slaves in *rebel* States shall be emancipated, and in the Border *loyal* States; but that the States shall be deprived of the power of upholding slavery, now or in the future. The emancipation of slaves now in the rebel States would be but one step in the process. To abolish slavery by the power of the National Government involves a fundamental change in the Constitution of the United States, by force of which "the right of each State to order and control its own domestic institutions, according to its own judgment," is taken away; a right which the Republican party has declared "*was essential to that balance of powers on which the perfection and endurance of our political fabric depends.*" This power of the State to regulate its internal police and domestic institutions is a vital, essential feature of our civil polity.

If it may be taken from the States to abolish slavery, it may be taken from them for any purpose. It is a question of power, and not merely of its use. The change involved is a change in the whole structure of the Government. The States and the union of States are gone. The result is, one State, one vast central power, a republic in name only. This fundamental change in our system of Government is to be wrought by the power of the sword, without action of States or people. This is the inauguration of a war of revolution wholly outside of the Constitution; a war, practically, for the entire subjugation and permanent conquest of fifteen States: for an attempt to destroy slavery by a revolution will unite the entire South against it. These fifteen States must be reduced to military colonies, and held in subjection by vast standing armies and by vast navies. If the thing were practicable, it would be at the cost of national exhaustion and the loss of our own freedom. You cannot maintain your conquest over fifteen subject States, covering so vast a territory, except by a military despotism. But the thing is impracticable. Every dollar spent for such a conquest would be wasted; every drop of blood shed for it would be spilt on the ground. The talk of a war of utter extermination is mere passion, which reason and conscience alike condemn. The only war the people desire is a war of restoration. If we go beyond this, we embark on a sea of strife and blood, without chart or compass; a war of vengeance and hate, of carnage and desolation, physical and moral, compared with which, all we have seen in the war thus far are ministrations of mercy.

Let me not be misunderstood. It is my firm conviction, that, in the prosecution of this war, the power of slavery will be broken; if the war shall be prolonged, utterly broken. Practically, the question of emancipation is one of *possessio pedis*. The Union army will not leave slavery behind it. Emancipation will not precede, but follow in its footsteps.

Ponder on these things, fellow-citizens. Stand by the Constitution; stand by the Union; stand by their glorious emblem, the banner of our love and pride. Give yourselves freely to the service of your country. The thought of her is in every heart, and on every lip; breaks into prayer, melts into tears, kindles into flame; the last thought at night, the first thought of morning: our country, perplexed, but not in despair; cast down, but not destroyed; wrestling with adversity, as Jacob with the angel, to wring from it its blessing; veiled and eclipsed as the sun, to come forth again with life and light and healing in its beams. Fellow-citizens, at an hour of such extreme peril as this, principles are every thing; parties and individuals, nothing. I have not taken, for many years, an active part in politics. My judicial position forbade it. I have had no direction of the "People's" movement; but I believe it had its origin in dissatisfaction with the existing condition of public affairs, in a natural and wise dread of any attempt to change the objects and purposes of the war, and in distrust of political cliques who have used the party in power for their own ends, and not for the country's. I cordially approve of the spirit and general objects of this movement. I know well, and respect and honor, gentlemen connected with it. I believe their apparent objects are their real objects. Truer men, more loyal and patriotic, are not found in the Commonwealth.

They are conservative in their views; but they are in favor of the vigorous prosecution of the war, of maintaining the nation's unity at every cost, and of cordially upholding the President in the discharge of his great and difficult duties. They cling with tenacity and unfaltering devotion to the Union and the Constitution of their fathers. Mistakes have doubtless been made; mistakes especially which show an ignorance of political machinery and management.

> "Where ignorance is bliss,
> 'Tis folly to be wise."

It is my firm conviction, that the certain result of the rigid, proscriptive, partisan policy adopted by the Republican Convention, especially if followed up by the charge of treason against all who dissent from it, is a divided North; divided not as to the duty of suppressing the Rebellion, but so divided in feeling and policy as to render efficient co-operation impracticable. I pray you, my Republican friends, to listen to the voices that come to us from the Great West, and to be tolerant and just. The men of Massachusetts cannot be driven. They will practise forbearance for their country's sake, but not for ever.

To what condition of things have we come, fellow-citizens, when such a man as Josiah G. Abbott can be denounced as a traitor, and this, too, as he stands by the fresh-made grave of a son, dearly beloved; one of three given to the service of his country? I know him well.

A man better qualified to represent you cannot be found in the district; and it is one of strong men. He is a very able lawyer; and great questions of law will have to be settled by the next Congress. He is a man of thoroughly practical mind, of large common sense, of extensive knowledge of men and business. He is a patriot through and through, from the crown of his head to the sole of his foot.

Nor can any charity excuse or palliate the gross attacks made upon the accomplished and gallant standard-bearer of this movement.* A leader at one of the ablest bars of the State, respected and beloved by his brethren, at the first call of his country he gave himself to her service. Beginning the war as major of a battalion, he has been successively appointed colonel, brigadier-general, and has now command of a division. His courage and gallantry have been tested; his ability is unquestioned, his character without reproach. How Christian gentlemen can denounce such men as traitors, it is difficult for a plain man to comprehend.

---

* Gen. Charles Devens.

REMARKS ON THE BORDER STATES.

HOUSE OF REPRESENTATIVES, JAN. 8, 1863.

The House being in Committee of the Whole, and having under consideration the Appropriation Bill, Mr. THOMAS said, —

Mr. CHAIRMAN, — I beg to call the attention of the Committee back to the precise matter before us. It is a provision for the appropriation of money for a definite and specific purpose: that purpose is, to enforce the collection of a direct tax assessed by Congress in conformity to a provision of the Constitution of the United States (art. 1, sect. 2, clause 4); a tax which could only have been assessed in exact conformity to that provision. The object of this provision in the appropriation bill, and of the law of the last session, is to enforce, in the disaffected States, the collection of the tax. Upon what ground, Mr. Chairman, are we seeking to enforce this tax in the "seceded" States? Upon the obvious ground, that the authority of this Government at this time is as valid over those States as it was before the acts of secession were passed; upon the ground, that every act of secession passed by those States is utterly null and void; upon the ground, that an act legally null and void cannot acquire force, because armed rebellion is behind it, seeking to uphold it; upon the ground, that the Constitution makes us, not a mere confederacy, but a nation; upon the ground, that the provisions of that Constitution strike through the State government, and reach directly, not intermediately, the subjects of the United States.

Gentlemen say that there is a belligerent power exercising authority against us. That is, you say that rebellion is attempting revolution. Very well. Who ever heard, as a matter of public law, that the authority of a government over its rebellious subjects was lost until that revolution was successful, was a fact accomplished? That day, I pray God, I may not live to see.

My position, then, Mr. Chairman, is, that we may enforce the collection of this tax, because to-day, as heretofore, the authority of the National Government binds and covers every inch of the national domain; because that law, which we call the Constitution, is, to-day, the supreme law of the land. If the position taken by the learned gentleman from Pennsylvania [Mr. Stevens] be true, that we are every day passing unconstitutional acts, we are every day violating our oaths to support the Constitution of the United States. I beg leave to say, that, however we may differ as to the extent of powers which the Constitution gives us (and they are ample for all good ends), when we deliberately pass from fidelity to this Constitution, to enact laws in violation of its sacred provisions, we are ourselves inaugurating revolution. It is fire against fire, revolution against revolution; and God have mercy on the country! In all events, at whatever cost or peril of treasure or of life, we must cling to the national unity; and, for this end, we must cling to the only possible bond of unity, the Constitution.

I have but a word more to say, Mr. Chairman. I have

listened quietly, but with great sorrow, to the attacks often made on the Republican side of the House against the gentlemen from the Border States. I desire to say, what I have often said, and repeat, with the fullest sense of my responsibility, that in fidelity to the Union and the Constitution, and every earnest effort to uphold them, there have been no truer, nobler, more devoted men than these representatives from the Border States. [Applause.] And the great heart of this country to-day goes out to meet them and to bless them. It is easy in New England (where fortunes are rapidly built up, and industry quickened, and material prosperity advanced, by this war), or in New York, or in Pennsylvania, to be patriotic and loyal and national. *These* men have stood the touch of fire and the sword. They have been tried by suffering. No ties of natural affection, no love of kindred, no fear of desolation or death, has moved them; not even your unkindness. I do not believe that it is policy or wisdom to alienate such men from us: we should rather grapple them with hooks of steel to our hearts.

Say what you will, Mr. Chairman, as a practical question, this war must be fought out in the Border States. They constitute the battle-ground of this contest to-day, as they have been from the beginning of the war. Can you hold the Border States to their allegiance? If you can, the final victory is with us; if you cannot, separation is inevitable. I hope and trust and pray, Mr. Chairman, that we shall hear no more of party discussions and wrangles; no more reproaches thrown from the one side of the House to the other. We have no strength thus to fritter away. God knows, we need a united people to save the Union, trembling, even now, on the verge of dissolution; and therefore, if we cannot agree upon all questions of law, if we cannot agree upon all questions of policy, let us consent to differ as we best may, but with the firm resolve, that every thing of strength, of power, of purpose, of motive, of will, that is in us, shall combine, concentrate, converge, to save the national integrity, the national life.

It has been said by the gentleman from Pennsylvania, — and I will say a word on this, and relieve your patience, — that there are those here who oppose the policy of the Administration. I suppose there is no man in this House who has more respect for the intellectual vigor and manliness of the gentleman from Pennsylvania [Mr. Stevens] than I have; but I beg leave to call his attention to the fact, that he has not always been able to concur in the policy of this Administration. I beg leave to remind him of a difficulty which has occurred to all members of the House, that it has sometimes been very difficult for even a very careful and scrutinizing observer to know or find out what the policy of the Administration is; and we are obliged to grope our way darkly therefore, and determine for ourselves what will be for the peace and interest of the country, and follow that. If the Administration does not clearly indicate its policy, we may be excused for not being always found in its path; and, when indicated, we may not follow it, if fidelity to the Constitution or the highest interests of the country forbid.

ON THE BILL "TO RAISE ADDITIONAL SOLDIERS FOR THE SERVICE OF THE GOVERNMENT."

HOUSE OF REPRESENTATIVES, JAN. 31, 1863.

I HAVE no desire, Mr. Speaker, to launch my bark upon the sea of this illimitable debate. My object in obtaining the floor last evening, was to present, in addition to a few remarks upon the bill before the House, some considerations concerning the relations of New England, and more especially what has been called the Puritanism of New England, to the Union. But I could not fail to see that this subject would be too remote from that immediately before the House. I propose, therefore, to confine myself to a few, I fear somewhat desultory, suggestions upon the measure before us, and the policy which it involves.

It seems to me, Mr. Speaker, that the discussion, thus far, has scarcely touched, much less carefully considered, the special subject-matter before us. This bill proposes, as I understand it, to raise a new and large army from the men of African descent in this country. The amendment offered by the gentleman from Pennsylvania [Mr. Stevens] to the original bill (the measure to be pressed) proposes to raise that army without limitation as to numbers; without limitation as to the States, loyal or rebel, from which they are to be taken; without limitation as to the expense, because without limitation as to number; without limitation as to the places where, or purposes for which, the army is to be used; without limitation as to the discipline to which that army is to be subjected; each and all of these matters resting solely in the discretion of the President of the United States. I believe that I shall have the concurrence of every member of this House, and of the gentleman from Pennsylvania [Mr. Stevens] among the rest, when I say, that this bill, in its new form, proposes to vest in the President of the United States a larger power and wider discretion than were ever reposed by Congress in the hands of one man, unless under our previous legislation on the same subject. I am not here, Mr. Speaker, to raise the question, whether we may not wisely repose a large discretion in the Executive at a time like this. It is among the necessities of our condition, that a large discretion should be reposed in the Executive; but it is the duty of Congress to see that no such extent of power is vested in the President, or any one else, that that power may be readily used, as all power is liable to be used, to defeat the ends for which it is given, to subvert instead of upholding the laws. And this question is not one of the individual character of the officer, but of principle and policy. In what condition of our affairs do we propose to raise this new army?

If I understood rightly the chairman of the Committee on Military Affairs, my friend from New York [Mr. Olin], we have now in the field, or rather we have upon the pay-rolls of the Government, a million of white men of the Anglo-Saxon, Celtic, or German races. This, no man can doubt, is a sufficient army for the purpose of suppressing this Rebellion, if this Rebellion can be subdued by physical power alone. I do not say how many of those men are engaged to-day in active service, in face of the enemy. There are, we are told, very large desertions from the army. There are vast numbers now on your pay-rolls, capable of service, who are doing no service. But that must be, to a considerable extent the fault of the administration of the army. It is the plain, obvious duty of the Government to see that these men, who are on your pay-rolls and capable of service, are rendering that service. With a million efficient men in the army and at work, and with our large and gallant navy, if it is practicable to conquer rebellion by arms, you have force adequate for the purpose; as large a force as we can hope to maintain and replenish without bankruptcy.

We must look, Mr. Speaker, to the financial aspect of this question, the question of ways and means. I do not think the financial condition of this country has been truly presented; or rather, I should say, fully presented: for no gentleman, of course, could desire to present it otherwise than truly. If I understand the facts spread by the gentlemen of the Committee of Ways and Means before the country, in the speeches made on this floor, our national debt at the end of the next fiscal year will be at the least two thousand million dollars. By that debt is meant the liquidated debt of the country. I would call the attention of the House to the fact, that the unliquidated debt of this country, the debt for damages for the taking of property and the destruction of property by the military power in the prosecution of the war, upon any equitable or reasonable rule which this Congress or any other Congress may adopt in its adjustment, may reach as high as five hundred millions more. This may be possibly too large an estimate; but gentlemen will see at once, that how large it may be, and whether it reaches this limit, must depend on the rule which Congress shall apply to the adjustment of those claims; how widely the door is thrown open. If we admit not only all legal claims, but all claims that are equitable, in the ordinary sense of that word, and if the estimate also include pensions, I think I do not state the case too strongly when I say it would reach five hundred millions.

Do not fail to observe one other fact of our financial condition; and that is, that when you get the national debt of this country, liquidated and unliquidated, you do not reach the whole marrow of the thing. Your state, county, city, town, and parish debts all over this country, taken together, will make an aggregate approaching at least to half of the liquidated national debt at the end of the present fiscal year; and when you combine these debts, the liquidated debt, the unliquidated debt, the liability for pensions, the State, county, city, and town debts, and consider also how much higher interest we are paying than that paid by any other people, the fact will stare you in the face, that this nation, at the end of the next fiscal year, will be more heavily laden with debt than any nation in Europe.

Now, I make no complaint of this, Mr. Speaker. I

would not withhold nor give grudgingly even my last dollar to the prosecution of this righteous war; righteous, if prosecuted for the ends for which it was begun, — the noblest war this country could wage; compared with which, the Revolution itself was not only on a small scale, but for ends less grand and momentous. I differ from some of my friends here as to the nature and object of this war. It is a pleasant thing to say this is a war for liberty. It sounds well; it soothes the ear; it stirs the blood: but it is not true. That is not the fundamental idea of this war. Liberty we have had, sometimes to license. The fundamental idea, the idea of highest moral dignity, in the prosecution of this war, is the upholding of civil order and law and the Constitution, which is the nation's supreme law, its bond of unity, and its breath of life; the noblest product of human thought; the framework of an empire capable of almost infinite expansion, in which central power was reconciled with local independence, the gentlest restraint with the highest security, the broadest equality with the firmest order, the amplest protection with the slightest burden. The thought of to-day is not liberty, as commonly understood, the absence of restraint; but the law in which true liberty is enthroned and made possible.

I repeat, Mr. Speaker, I do not groan under the burdens the country has been and will be called to bear in the just prosecution of the war. It may be (though that question is now one of history only), it may be, that, by early mutual restraint and by moderate counsels, the war might have been averted. But it was not begun by this Government. After the first shot at Sumter, it was an inevitable necessity, a war of self-defence. I am yet in favor of vigorously prosecuting the war until the ends for which it was instituted are attained, or their attainment clearly seen to be impossible. I am for prosecuting it by the use of all just means and instruments, all means and instruments which have the sanction of public law as it has been tempered by civilization and Christianity.

But to the *money* aspect of the question: the bill, without disturbing the present army at all, without diminution of its numbers, authorizes the President of the United States to enlist one hundred thousand, or two hundred thousand, or three hundred thousand men of African descent; and every new man you put into your army, according to the estimates of intelligent gentlemen on the floor of this House, costs you from seven hundred to a thousand dollars; and if you raise one hundred and fifty thousand men, as was proposed by the gentleman from Pennsylvania originally, you increase your expenses one hundred to one hundred and fifty millions a year.

Mr. STEVENS. The gentleman will allow me a word. I understand him to say, that this bill proposes to raise an additional army, without any diminution in the number of the present army. Now, the preamble to the bill which I introduced stated expressly, that it was upon the ground, that, within a few months, the terms of enlistment of several hundred thousand of the troops now in the field would expire; and this proposes to supply their places.

Mr. THOMAS. That was in the preamble of the original bill introduced by the gentleman from Pennsylvania; but the bill reported as from the War Department, and now before the House, has no such provision. The authority vested in the President, according to his construction of our statutes, is to raise an army of a million men. I do not complain of that construction. There is no provision in this bill for the diminution of that number; and that number is not to be diminished, at any rate, until June next. I may add, a bill has been introduced in the other end of the Capitol for the recruiting of this army, and supplying its losses.

Mr. Speaker, let me now turn to another feature of this bill, the *term* of enlistment. It provides for the enlistment of men for a period of *five* years. Why *five* years? I think there is more significance in that word " five " in this bill than in all other *words* written in it. Its possible objects are not written. Do you mean to say to the country, that it is your expectation, your reasonable expectation, and the basis on which you propose to make enlistments for your army, that this war is to continue for a period of five years longer? Do you mean to say to the country, that on the vast scale on which the war is now prosecuted, and at the expense of treasure and of life at which it is prosecuted, you expect to carry it on for five years more? If such be your expectation, it is just and manly to say so. If such be not your expectation, pray add nothing to the anxiety and alarm of the people.

Mr. Speaker, if the object of this war is restoration, that involves a state of things, present or future, which will soon be developed and felt. A war for restoration proceeds upon the ground, that you will find in the rebel States, as your army advances and protection is made possible, men who are ready to rally again under the blessed flag of the Union, and to return to their allegiance to the National Government. If that feeling exists, and is developed, certainly it will be developed before the lapse of five years; never, indeed, by *this* instrumentality; never! But if the object of this war is not restoration; if the purpose and object of this war are, as is sometimes declared in the heated and brilliant rhetoric of gentlemen on your left, subjugation, extermination, the re-colonization of the whole rebel territory, then your term of enlistment is altogether too short, altogether too short.

If, Mr. Speaker, the object be extermination, there is not one of these pages, snatched prematurely from his mother's arms or cradle, who will live to see the end. You have been waging the war two years, and yet the number of inhabitants in the rebel States to-day is larger than it was when the war was begun. You cannot, probably, if you would, and you would not if you could, carry on a war with a fierceness and severity that would destroy life as rapidly as it germinates. Men, in war even, will marry, and women be given in marriage; children will be born to them, and their mothers will hold them to their flowing breasts as the storm sweeps by. The angel of life will triumph over the angel of death. Such is the blessed economy of God. The extermination of eight millions of people, with the use of all our power and all our resources, is a moral and physical impossibility. Of this war, if it is carried on for extermination, neither you nor I, Mr. Speaker, may hope to see its close but in one way, to us the way of deepest humiliation, — the intervention of other nations to stay its ravages. Who talks of a war of extermination is simply mad.

I proceed, Mr. Speaker, to a consideration of the *material* of which you propose to make up this army. If I understand myself, I entertain very little prejudice and no unkindness toward the colored race. I may believe, I do believe, as a matter of fact, that, in the sterner stuff, they are an inferior race; in some of the gentler qualities, our superiors; and, in my judgment, the moral condemnation of slavery is the sterner for that fact. I have more respect, or rather less aversion, hate, for Roman or Grecian slavery, which subdued equals to its service, not inferiors; not men to whom Nature had not given equal power of self-reliance and self-protection. But I also believe, that as society now exists, where these races are brought together in numbers approaching equality, the relations that will exist between them, *will* be, perhaps *must* be, to some extent, relation of dependence and pupilage on the one part, and government and protection on the other; but not involving necessarily any feature of chattel slavery.

Now, I do not enter into the philosophy of races. As a practical man, I take and deal with things as they are. Looking at the existing relations in different parts of the country between the two races, I believe, after much reflection and careful consideration, that as matter of wisdom, for the good of both, and especially for the permanent good of the colored race, we should not involve that race in this war if we can fairly avoid it. To some extent, and for valuable services, they have been and will be used; but, in the policy of creating from them distinct and large armies, we shall lose more than we gain. They will fight by the side of their masters better than they will against them. This may seem strange at first blush; but, the more you study the African character, the firmer will be your conviction of its soundness. The light which our history gives us is mainly of slaves fighting with their masters; and the fact will be found to be, though not, of course, without its exceptions, that slaves are attached and devoted to their masters and their families, and will stand by them, and fight with and for them.

I do not question that there are men of color in this country capable of bearing arms and making good soldiers. There are men of talent and culture among them. I have heard a man of color in this country address a polished assembly with a beauty of style, and force of argument, which any gentleman on the floor of this House might be content to equal; which I should be glad to imitate. But, Mr. Speaker, great questions of public policy are not determined rightly on exceptional cases: they confirm rather than impair the rule. And no valuable judgment can be formed as to the usefulness of a negro army of a hundred thousand men from the fact that a hundred men here, or fifty men there, had been used in the military service, and had been used successfully. The practical question is, taking one, two, or three hundred thousand of escaped slaves from the rebel and border States, what sort of material you have for an army, compared with the present material?

My friend from New York [Mr. Roscoe Conkling] has caused to be read some remarks of Alexander Hamilton on this subject. There is no statesman in our history for whom I have a profounder respect; but I have no confidence in the views expressed as to the proper material of an army, as applied to the times in which we live, or the purposes for which the war is waged. The argument proceeds on the ground, that the soldier is, to all practical intents and purposes, a machine. Mr. Speaker, the soldier of to-day is a thinking, or, if you will, " a calculating machine." Your army in the field, as the history of this war will signally illustrate, is valuable for your service just in the degree that it is intelligent; just in the degree that your soldiers are capable of understanding and appreciating the duty which they have to perform, and the fealty which they owe to the Government; just in the degree that the man within inspires and animates and nerves and presses onward the outer man; just in the degree that he feels that this glorious country and beneficent Government are his country and his Government, the life-estate in him, the fee in his children. Suppose, for example (I hope my friend from Maine, listening to me, will take no offence), you get a regiment of backwoodsmen of Maine, men inured to life in boreal airs, whose stalwart arms humble forests: you have an excellent regiment, because the backwoodsmen of Maine are thinking, intelligent men, owning the country, and loving it. Take an equal number of young men from one of our cities, of culture and spirit and pride, and you would have at least as good soldiers. Nay, more: if you were to take these two bodies of men, and cross with them the Rocky Mountains, you would find that the young men from the city, of intelligence and spirit, would bear all the fatigues, privations, and hardships, as well as the stoutest woodmen; "better," said to me one who had tried the experiment, — Capt. Williams, of the Second Massachusetts Regiment, one of the many noble offerings Massachusetts has freely laid on the altar of country.

Mr. Hamilton cites the authority of Frederick of Prussia, a great soldier and loose talker: yet we may concede, that, for many uses to which armies have been put, it were well to have them as near to machines as possible; the nearer the better. Stupidity might, to some extent, be compensated by unthinking obedience to the will of the commander. Such an army this country does not seek, and will not have. Create an army of three hundred thousand men, so stupid as to understand nothing of the purpose for which the war is prosecuted; obedient, but obedient only to the will of a commander; mere "machines" in his hands; and they may be the readiest instruments to destroy what all good men are struggling to preserve.

For one, Mr. Speaker, I do not object to the enlistment of intelligent free men of color, though I doubt whether they seek it. I am a citizen of a State which recognizes the substantial equality of all men before the law. I love and honor her for her fidelity to the cause of freedom, though I may sometimes fear " she oves not wisely, but too well." I thank God, there is not a man treading the soil of Massachusetts who is not in all substantial legal rights my peer. The colored man of Massachusetts is as much a citizen of Massachusetts as I am. The question has been settled from our first Constitution. Nothing is clearer as matter of principle or of history; nor has there ever been any decision of the courts of the United States that impairs his right.

But, while I rejoice in the policy of Massachusetts toward the colored race, I do not assume to direct or control or curse the policy of other co-equal States. I am not unmindful of the fortunate condition, as to the colored race, in which the Revolution found us. I am not blind to the fact, that their numbers were so small as not to constitute practically a disturbing element. I am grateful for these things: but I am not sure, that if a half or a third of our population had been of African descent, and our soil and its products and their labor congenial, we should have been so much wiser and better than our neighbors; nor am I certain, that if we bordered on the slave States, and were exposed to the incoming of large numbers of black men, we should be so tolerant in our policy, though we should try to be just.

I do not form my judgment from the relations that exist between the white and colored races in Massachusetts, of those that must and should exist in States where the colored men constitute a large component part of the population; nor do I form a judgment, from my knowledge of some respectable and intelligent colored people at home, what sort of an army could be made up of the slave population of the South. Congress must recognize and act upon facts as they are, and not as they would have them to be. It must make large allowance for the feelings and prejudices even of the present army; yes, for the blind, unreasoning prejudices and hostilities of color and of race. Other generations may be wiser, better, more tolerant, than our own; but we have to *deal with our own.*

The friends of this measure are very confident, they are rather used to being confident, that these black men, slaves or freed, will make good soldiers. I cannot aver with certainty, they will not; but I can say, we have no satisfactory evidence that they will. I can say, that they lack the intelligence, the energy, and the self-reliance which characterize so largely our present army, and which all men have conceded to be the strength and effective power of that army.

But suppose that the experiment you are to try is not successful. Suppose you raise an army of two or three hundred thousand men of African descent, and you find that the capacity is not in them which free institutions have given to your white soldiers, the spirit and habit of self-reliance and self-possession; and I may remark in passing, Mr. Speaker (I suppose there is no man in this House who has not lived long enough to have learned it), that the great difference between men in this world is the degree in which they possess themselves, — their own powers and resources. Suppose, I repeat, that your experiment should fail, and you have this army of two or three hundred thousand black men on your hands: what will you do with them? If you have an army composed of the white citizens of the country, and the period of their service expires, they will return to the ordinary relations and avocations of life and business; they will resume their former position in society. They are soldiers to-day: they are citizens to-morrow. But an army of two or three hundred thousand black men, freed slaves, to be disbanded, where shall they go? To what place and condition are they to be returned? Of course, not to slavery. No man who has ever served under our flag, whether for a day or for an hour, can be made again a slave. Where, then, shall they go? You may be willing to colonize them; but they may prefer not to be colonized. I wish some practical man, who is disposed to discuss these questions upon practical grounds, would tell me what disposition you would make of these men, if the experiment fails, as fail I believe it will; or when their term of service has expired.

Mr. Speaker, I have listened attentively to this debate. I think I may claim the merit, if I have no other, of being a very patient listener; and it sometimes requires a patience which Job himself would envy. But every thing affecting, ever so remotely, the destiny of the country, is of painful interest now. I have, with pleasure for the most part, listened to this discussion. It has concerned great principles of policy and of conduct in the administration of our affairs. But I deeply regret to have seen the spirit of party so often invoked in this debate. It has no place in the presence of these great perils and great duties. The utmost freedom of discussion and of counsel, here and elsewhere, must be maintained. Principles are vital; party organizations or triumphs, individual hopes and aspirations, nothing. That party will wear the crown which shall do most to save the life of this nation, its unity, its liberty in law. No party can hope to triumph which is not faithful to these great aims; unless the triumph of its policy and the ruin of the country shall be cotemporaneous.

I heard with great sorrow the thoughtful and eloquent speech of the gentleman from Kansas; but I heard it with no *surprise*. It was but carrying out the principles laid down in his speech a year ago to their plainest and most logical conclusion. The principles were received with cordial sympathy and warmest welcome by men who shrink from the conclusion as from the abyss of despair. He and they rejected with scorn the old Union, any Union, with slave States. The only alternatives were revolution and permanent conquest of the entire South, or separation. The first is felt to be impossible; and the gentleman from Kansas logically, and I have no doubt honestly, accepts the alternative. But the gentleman cannot fail to see that the question before the country to-day is, not *separation* or no, but *disintegration* or no; that, the moment you sever the bond as to one State, you sever it as to the whole. No man can say, if separation begins, where it will end, or where the division-line will ultimately fall. Our only safety has been and is in clinging to the Union as it was in fact, and still is *de jure;* the old Union, the blessed Union of our fathers.

It has been clear to me as the sun in heaven and at

mid-day, that this was our only possible way of salvation. This old Constitution, spurned now by foot even of sciolist and charlatan, this stone the builders of "baseless fabrics" have rejected, must again become the head of the corner. I beseech and adjure statesmen at either end of the Capitol, at either end of the Avenue, to continue no policy, to enter upon none, which shall preclude the restoration of the Union, with the rights and powers of the States unimpaired; the only Union now within the reach, even of hope.

I regret deeply some of the measures of the Administration. I have earnestly, and with a depth of conviction which could find no adequate utterance, protested against them. The confiscation bill, the proclamations of Sept. 22d and 24th and Jan. 1st, powerless for good, have been, and will be, I fear, fruitful only of evil.

The proclamation of Sept. 24th is in conflict with the august and sacred muniments of personal security, to which, for six centuries, the Anglo-Saxon mind and heart have clung as the gospel of civil freedom. Every arrest made under it in the loyal and peaceful States serves only to strengthen the enemies of the Government, and to wound and grieve its friends. If they tried to say "Amen" to it, the amen would stick in their throats. Pray, let it sleep "the sleep that knows no waking."

The proclamation of Jan. 1st will do less good or harm than its friends hoped or opponents feared. It is not thus that great wars are prosecuted or great ends accomplished. However kind may have been the motives of those who begat and conceived it, it was stillborn; and no political galvanism can give to it the semblance of life. But though the Administration may adopt measures my judgment condemns, having attempted to stay them, and protested against them, I stand in the path of duty. This is my country to serve, my Government to obey, my Constitution to rescue and save, my Union,

> "Where I have garnered up my heart;
> Where I must live, or bear no life."

Amid all the darkness, the thick darkness, around us, I cling to the single, simple, sublime issue, the Constitution, and the Union of which it is the bond; the old Union. God bless the old Union, and the wrath of the Lamb of God shrivel to their very sockets the arms lifted to destroy it; — not in vengeance, but in mercy to them and to all mankind!

This country of ours, this nation of ours, is the grandest, sublimest trust that was ever committed into human hands. Pray the Father of lights, we be faithful. My way of duty, in one regard, has been plain: having sworn to support the Constitution of the United States, I have striven to keep the oath. The way of obvious duty was, in my judgment, the way, the only way, of wisdom and safety for the country.

It was the prayer of New England's greatest statesman, that, when his eyes were turned for the last time to behold the sun of heaven, he might not see him shining on the broken and dishonored fragments of a *once* glorious Union. Have we ever repeated to ourselves these words, "*once* glorious," "*once* glorious Union"?

Then with tears let us wash out, or with fire burn out, the word, and write "*for ever* glorious," born out of tribulation into a nobler life. When our eyes shall turn to behold for the last time the sun in heaven, may we see his rays kindling every star and every stripe of that banner, which, like the robe of our divine Master, was woven without seam!

If we save this Union, generation after generation will rise up to bless us. If we lose it through divisions, through party strifes, through supineness, in seeking other ends, our memories will rot evermore.

THE LOUISIANA ELECTION CASES.

HOUSE OF REPRESENTATIVES, FEB. 16, 1863.

Mr. SPEAKER, — Whatever other differences of opinion there may be between members of this House, we all recognize the great importance of the principles and policy involved in the resolutions before us. There are certain facts that are not contested. It is not contested in the report of the Committee, or in the arguments of the members of the Committee of Elections who did not sign the report, that the persons who are elected to this House are loyal men. It is not contested, that they were elected by loyal citizens of Louisiana. It is not contested, that they were elected without military dictation or control. There is nothing developed in the report or in the arguments presented to the House to show that there was any military dictation or control or influence in the election.

What are the relations which these electors, and the persons who claim these seats, hold, at this moment, to the Government of the United States? They are citizens of the United States, subject to all the duties imposed by the Constitution and laws of the United States. They are subject to taxation. Since the ordinance of secession was passed, they have been taxed, in conformity to the provision of the Constitution (art. 1, sect. 2) which apportions direct taxation. They are subject to your revenue-laws. Your collector is there to-day collecting duties imposed by the Government. They are subject to your excise-duties. Your law passed at the last session applies to and includes them. They are subject to military service. Some four thousand of loyal residents of New Orleans are already engaged in the military service of the Government.

Now, Mr. Speaker, before the act of secession, these men had all the political rights that are correlative to these political duties. They had the right of representation, which, from the earliest history of this Government, has been indissolubly connected with the right of taxation. Subject, in war or peace, to all the duties and burdens of the Government, they are entitled to the corresponding rights and privileges that Government had conferred upon them, unless in some legal way deprived of them. These propositions are too plain for argument.

I proceed, then, Mr. Speaker, to consider whether these rights have been in any way modified or impaired by the act of secession. Were they impaired by the ordinance passed by the convention of Louisiana? It is conceded on all hands, that that act was null and void, and that it did not change the relations which the State of Louisiana sustained to this Union. Is that act of secession, in itself null and void, rendered operative and effective by the use of physical power or armed force? Or, to state the proposition in another form, is the ordinance of secession rendered effective because armed treason is behind it? Very clearly, no. An act, void in itself under the supreme law of the land, cannot be made to affect or impair the legal rights of any, the humblest citizen, because armed treason seeks to enforce it.

Mr. Speaker, this doctrine is, I know, contested; but I venture to say, that there is no form in which the proposition, that the seceded States have committed either suicide or treason, can be put, in which its absurdity is not transparent. That I may do no injustice to the advocates of this doctrine, I will read the statement of it made by my distinguished colleague [Mr. Eliot]; and I beg the House to mark the force and effect of his words. He is speaking of the ordinance of secession; and he says,

"But being of no effect by law, yet operative and vitalized by false form of law, and by effective and controlling force in fact, it followed inevitably, that, while the rebel State had renounced its allegiance and cast off the protection of the Government, its territory remained within the Union; and its loyal men thereupon residing were entitled to protection in their persons and in their property, and in all their rights, as soon as the military power of the Government could be exerted there, and a new civil government within the State could be created."

That is to say, the proposition of my colleague is, that, although the act of secession is void by law, " it is vitalized by a false form of law," and by the force behind that false form of law. I may be very obtuse; but I prefer the plainer and simpler proposition, that an act which is utterly void by the supreme law of the land cannot be vitalized or made effective by armed treason, but is void still. And I beg leave, with all due deference to my distinguished colleague, to say, that, if that is the proposition which he told us the other day a majority of the sensible men of Massachusetts believe in, they have done great injustice to the foolish men of Massachusetts [laughter]; for they have robbed them of their appropriate food, and of the most absurd proposition they could find to believe in [laughter].

Mr. ELIOT. Will my colleague yield to me?

Mr. THOMAS. With pleasure.

Mr. ELIOT. Mr. Speaker, I was somewhat surprised the other day to observe how very sensitive my distinguished colleague was at the use which I then made of the word "sensible." But, when a gentleman states that a majority of sensible men are of a certain opinion, it does not by any means follow, that those who hold the adverse opinion may not also be sensible. My learned colleague must not suppose that I intended at all to place him in the category of those who were not sensible, certainly not; but only among the minority of sensible men [laughter]. My learned colleague is as sensible as any of those who differ from him. I should be the last man to take from him any claim which he, certainly with some sensitiveness, seems to assert, that he belongs to a sensible party. In Massachusetts, I am glad to believe, it is a party in the minority, although there are in it very sensible gentlemen.

Mr. THOMAS. I cannot yield the floor to a speech. If my colleague desires to ask a question or to make an explanation, I have no objection.

Mr. ELIOT. I am endeavoring to make an explanation; and I began on that point because my colleague has been so very sensitive. Two or three times he referred to it as though I intended to intimate that he and the People's party in Massachusetts were not sensible. Far be it from me to say that they are not sensible men. In that particular, however, I think they are decidedly in the minority; and, so far as the questions are concerned that divided the People's party from the great body of men in Massachusetts last fall, I cannot, from my stand-point, believe that they were as sensible as I hope my learned friend will be when he comes next to the polls.

Mr. THOMAS. I cannot yield the floor to my colleague to make a political speech.

Mr. ELIOT. My colleague must keep good-natured.

Mr. THOMAS. It is not surely a question of good nature. Mine is not easily exhausted; but I desire to proceed with my remarks. I do not desire to hear a talk about the People's party or any other party. Graver matters are before us.

Mr. ELIOT. Does my friend decline to yield the floor?

Mr. THOMAS. For a political speech, I must. If my colleague has any explanation he desires to make, I will yield for explanation; but I cannot yield for a speech.

Mr. ELIOT. I desire to make an explanation. Mr. Speaker, I do not know whether that phrase, "State suicide," originated in this House or in the other branch of Congress. It is not a phrase that to my mind conveys a clear and distinct state of facts. I have never used it. My learned colleague has attributed it to me. I repeat, I have never used it. I have entertained the idea, and now entertain a distinct idea, of what I have called State treason. I had the honor to speak upon that subject last summer; and it was in the course of that speech that I stated, more at large than I can now do, what seem to me to be the true doctrines on that subject.

Mr. THOMAS. I cannot yield the floor and my time for this discussion.

Mr. ELIOT. It takes some little time to explain my point.

Mr. THOMAS. I do not desire to give up my time for discussion upon this question, and I must decline further to yield the floor.

Mr. ELIOT. Very well: then I will just say——

The Speaker *pro tempore*. The gentleman from Massachusetts is not in order. His colleague declines to yield the floor.

Mr. ELIOT. My colleague yields to me, as I understand, to finish this statement.

The Speaker *pro tempore*. Does the gentleman from Massachusetts yield the floor?

Mr. THOMAS. For my colleague to finish what he was saying at the moment.

Mr. ELIOT. When a State has done what, under the language of the Constitution, amounts to treason; when it has given aid and comfort to the enemy; when it has levied war against the Government; when its Governor has abdicated, its Legislature gone over to the enemy; when it has, by all the forms of law, arrayed itself against the Government; I say, that State has committed treason, and that, as such, it has forfeited all its rights as a State, leaving the loyal men of the State to be cared for and protected by the Government. But I repeat, that, as a corporation, it has committed treason, and has forfeited all its rights under the Government as a traitor State.

Mr. THOMAS. Is this all my colleague has to say?

Mr. ELIOT. Just to finish the sentence. And may be declared by the Government as having forfeited all its rights and privileges as a State.

Mr. THOMAS. The doctrine, then, is, that a State cannot hang itself, but may put itself in a state of preparation to be hanged.

Mr. ELIOT. It deserves to be hanged.

Mr. THOMAS. It can, of course, be arraigned for treason; it can be indicted for treason, brought to trial before a jury of its peers for treason, and hung for treason [laughter]. The statement well illustrates what I have before stated, that there is no form of words into which you can put this doctrine that its absurdity will not be transparent. The proposition commits suicide, not the State. *It is felo de se.* A State cannot commit treason; nor can the void act of a State change the relation which loyal citizens sustain to the United States; nor are the relations which loyal and obedient citizens sustain to the Government of the United States broken or severed because the ordinances of secession are backed up by traitors in arms. These citizens of Louisiana, therefore, hold the same legal relation to the United States that they did before the acts of secession and treason, by men wearing the garb of State authority, were committed.

The State of Louisiana exists; its functions may be in abeyance. All the powers of the State exist; and all that is necessary is simply that the machinery of the

State shall be put in motion. The State itself is like Milton's angels, which,

> "Vital in every part,
> Cannot but by annihilating die."

This, then, Mr. Speaker, is the state of things before us: The loyal men of these two districts of Louisiana, holding unbroken their legal relations to the Government of the United States, have elected representatives to this Congress of the United States; and the question is, Shall they be admitted? If not, why not? An objection has been made, though not much pressed, that there were no vacancies to fill. Vacancies existed by reason of the failure to elect at the general election, and those vacancies have never been filled. There is no one occupying a seat in this House from either of these two districts, because there have been no persons entitled by law to fill either of them. A case arose in which vacancies should be filled in pursuance of writs issued by executive authority of the State of Louisiana. Were they so issued?

I do not mean to say that this question is free from difficulty: it certainly is not. But it has been, I think, quite too summarily disposed of by gentlemen, opposed to the resolutions of the Committee. It seems to me, Mr. Speaker, that much, very much, of the difficulty we have in the discussion of this and similar questions, results from the attempt to apply to the condition of things in which we are placed, principles and rules from writers upon international law that really throw no light upon, and have no just application to, that condition, in many respects *sui generis;* and for our guide in which, history and public law furnish no precedents or even strong analogies. No just or reasonable conclusion can be drawn from the powers of a military governor, in a territory conquered from a foreign enemy, as to the nature and extent of the powers to be exercised in States, or parts of States, rescued from the possession of rebels in arms against us. This is a military occupation of our own territory; an occupation which has become necessary by reason of the fact, that the Constitution and laws of the United States cannot otherwise be enforced; and that it is our duty to enforce them, and the right of the loyal citizens of Louisiana to have them enforced, not merely for our benefit, but for their protection.

Now, Mr. Speaker, what is the object of this vast movement of ours? For what are we carrying on this war? For the purpose of enforcing the laws of the United States. Your war has no other just or legitimate object but the enforcement of your laws. If these laws are obstructed by armed force in the State of Louisiana, you have the right to take and to maintain military occupation of that State to remove such obstruction. You have the right to see that the laws of the United States are executed in the State of Louisiana.

Do gentlemen say, that, because of the existence of armed rebellion in the State of Louisiana, we have no right to enforce the laws of the United States there? Have not we the right to collect taxes? Have we not the right to enforce the revenue-laws, and the right to conscript soldiers from the citizens of that State? Have you not the right, by military power, to protect the courts of the United States in the district of Louisiana

the exercise of their jurisdiction? I take this po-
[si]tion, and I fail to see how it can be controverted,
[tha]t if you are in the military occupation of this, your
[ow]n territory, you hold it for the purpose for which the
[wa]r is waged; for the purpose of upholding the jurisdic-
[tio]n, and enforcing obedience to the laws, of the United
[St]ates.

The analogies sought to be drawn from Vattel, or
[oth]er writers on public law, as to the military occupation
[of] a conquered territory from a foreign State, have very
[im]perfect application to the case before us. The Consti-
[tu]tion and the laws of the United States are the supreme
[la]w of Louisiana, and you are to enforce the execution
[of] those laws; and I see no valid distinction between
[en]forcing those laws which impose duties and burdens
[up]on the people, and the enforcement of those laws
[wh]ich guarantee and protect the rights of the loyal people
[of] the State; rights springing from us, and to be pro-
[te]cted by us.

Mr. CONWAY. Was the law under which these men
[we]re elected a law of the United States?

Mr. THOMAS. The law from which the right to elect
[wa]s derived, and to be elected, was a law of the United
[St]ates, and the supreme law of Louisiana. Mr. Speaker,
[I] wish to make matters clear as I go. I want gentlemen,
[wh]o believe that we should enforce the laws of the
[U]nited States for the collection of taxes and the collec-
[tio]n of the revenue in Louisiana, to point out the dis-
[tin]ction between enforcing the laws of the United States
[wh]ich impose these burdens and duties upon the people,
[an]d the enforcing of the laws which secure to them the

enjoyment of their rights and privileges under the Constitution, and especially this great and invaluable right of representation, of helping to make the laws which they are bound to obey. Our duty to protect is as clear as their duty to obey. They are reciprocal and interdependent.

We may meet this question of the issue of writs of election in another manner. The question, whether these writs were properly issued or not, is a technical question, and we can meet it by a technical answer. We may meet the objection, that the writs were not issued by the executive authority of the State, by saying that they were issued by the only executive authority of that State which the Government of the United States or the people in these districts in any way recognize, and which, in matters of highest concern, they have recognized and obeyed. The writs of election were, in fact, issued upon the earnest request of the loyal citizens of these districts, and were responded to and confirmed by them.

But I do not consider the strict legality of these writs vital to the issue before us. I go one step further. I contend, whether these writs were issued by the executive authority of the State or not, this may be a valid election. I contend, that this provision of the Constitution, as other provisions of statute in relation to this subject, is within the well-settled distinction between provisions which are directory and those which are essential. I say, under the law of elections, practised upon from the beginning of the Government to this hour, you have gone behind the mere form to get at the substance and truth of the thing; and that these safeguards, provided by the laws to secure to the citizens the orderly exercise of the right of election, were never intended to be used as barriers to exclude them from their enjoyment. Let me call the attention of the House to elections whose validity this House has recognized, and which proceed upon this distinction.

Mr. PORTER. If I understand the gentleman from Massachusetts, he asserts, that, there being no Governor of Louisiana elected in pursuance of the provisions of her constitution and laws, the military commandant appointed by the President, who has assumed the title of Military Governor, is to be regarded as the Governor or executive authority of the State within the meaning of that clause of the Federal Constitution which provides, that, in case of vacancies in the representation of a State, the " executive authority thereof" shall issue writs of election.

Mr. THOMAS. I do not state the proposition so broadly as that. What I have said is, that we are in the military occupation of our own territory, a portion of it where the laws of the United States have been impeded by armed force; that we are there to enforce the laws of the United States; and that it is difficult to draw a sound distinction between the powers effective for the enforcement of the laws imposing burdens and duties upon the subject, and those which may be used for his protection. The gentleman is mistaken in his facts. Mr. Shepley did not assume the title of Military Governor. He was appointed Military Governor by the President.

Mr. PORTER. It seems to me that the gentleman is at fault in saying there is any law of the United States, so far as relates to the election of representatives in Congress, to be enforced. The Constitution says,

> "The times, places, and manner of holding elections for senators and representatives shall be prescribed in each State by the Legislature thereof; but the Congress may at any time, by law, make or alter such regulations, except as to the places of choosing senators."

When Congress shall have passed a law prescribing the time, place, and manner of electing representatives, then the military power may be invoked to remove obstructions in the way of carrying it into practical effect.

Mr. THOMAS. The provision of the Constitution cited by my friend from Indiana is the one referring to the *general* elections of representatives, and not to the elections to fill *vacancies*. It is by no means clear that any legislation of Congress could remove the difficulty. In case of vacancies in the delegation of any State, the Constitution says "the executive authority thereof shall issue writs of election to fill such vacancies." The legislation of Congress cannot supersede or modify this provision; and after legislation, as before, the same questions would arise as now. Is there an executive authority of the State, within the meaning of this provision? Is it sufficient that the writ is issued by one claiming to exercise the executive authority, with the recognition of this Government and with the assent of the people? Or is it our duty to go behind his certificate and action, and inquire, in a case where there is no conflicting claim or contest, as to the regularity of his appointment? And lastly, supposing that we were satisfied the authority was not regular; yet if a day was fixed, was known to all the voters, and the case shows they complied with the notice, and exercised the right of election fully and freely, must we or ought we to declare the election void because the authority issuing the writ was not regular?

Mr. PORTER. The learned gentleman will see to what a dangerous conclusion his argument must necessarily lead him. The Constitution provides, that, " when vacancies happen in the representation from any State, the executive authority thereof shall issue writs of election to fill such vacancies." There is also, however, another provision as to senators, that, "if vacancies happen by resignation or otherwise during the recess of the Legislature of any State, the executive thereof may make temporary appointments until the next meeting of the Legislature, which shall then fill such vacancy." The same words, " executive thereof," are employed in both cases; so that, from the argument of the gentleman, it must necessarily follow, that the military governor appointed by the President may fill vacancies in the Senate of the United States. Surely no one would be willing to allow such an exercise of power.

Mr. THOMAS. I do not think such a conclusion necessarily or legitimately follows. There is a broad distinction between the exercise of an official and judicial judgment in selecting a senator, and the exercise of a power in appointing a day for the people to select their own representatives. It has not been the uniform practice of the House to hold that these writs shall be issued by the executive authority of the State. I call attention to the fact, that gentlemen have been allowed to take, and now hold, seats upon this floor, under the acts of the Provisional Convention and Governor of Virginia. I call attention also to the fact, that uniformly elections have been held in the Territories before their admission as States into the Union, and where, therefore, the elections were held without the action of State authorities.

Mr. PORTER. I would suggest to the gentleman from Massachusetts, that that power has been exerted solely under the third section of the fourth article of the Constitution, providing that "new States may be admitted by the Congress into this Union." That clause has been interpreted to include the right to have all the officers at the time of admission necessary to represent the State in the Federal Congress.

Mr. THOMAS. Be it so; but that provision does not abrogate the other provision of the Constitution, which provides that the times and places for elections shall be fixed by the *Legislature* of the State. The practice bends the form to the substance. The House, by a large majority, during the present term, determined that an election held at a time not fixed by the Legislature of the State, but in the constitution of the State, was a valid election, though clearly a departure from the letter of the law.

The point to which I was endeavoring to lead the House is the distinction between those provisions formal and directory and those that I deem essential; and that the House, in the exercise of its power to judge of the elections and the returns of its members, has always felt itself enabled to go behind the "letter which killeth to the spirit which maketh alive," and to ascertain whether, in point of fact, there has been a fair election by the people of the district, having full opportunity to vote, and without violence or fraud. And, therefore, if gentlemen differ as to the authority of a military governor, or, as I would call him, the provisional governor, of a State, they may still be satisfied that there was a full and fair notice to the people of the election; and that the loyal people of those districts, having had such full and fair notice, did meet and freely exercise their elective franchise.

I beg leave to make this further obvious suggestion to the House: that you cannot expect, in districts like those in Louisiana, or in any other of the States whose citizens have been in arms against us, that regularity, or that adherence to the forms of law, which you may justly demand in a State where the operation of the laws has not been obstructed by force of arms. Irregularities are inevitable; and this House, under its power to determine the election of members, will see, not whether all the customary provisions of law have been complied with, but whether, in point of fact, there has been a fair and just election. Do sticking-in-the-bark gentlemen tell us the registry law was not complied with, and that, therefore, this election is void? It is a fact, that this provision for a registry law for New Orleans was embodied in the constitution of Louisiana adopted in 1852. It is also a fact, that there were two elections of representatives from New Orleans, of members admitted to seats in this

House, before any registry law had been passed. And upon what ground? Upon the plain ground, that you are not to deprive the electors of the exercise of this most important right of representation because there is a failure to comply with formal provisions of law. Suppose, for instance, the law required a check-list, and a check-list was not used in the election, and yet, upon a full investigation of the facts, the House is satisfied a man was elected by a clear majority, and without fraud or violence: there can be no question, that, under the power vested in the House, it would look directly to the merits of the election, and confirm it.

The distinguished gentleman from Indiana [Mr. Voorhees], who first spoke upon this subject, averred that there was great danger from the admission of these claimants, and, in like cases, that the executive authority of this Government would finally prevail over the rights and powers of the House. The answer to all such suggestions is to be found in the fidelity of this House to its rights, to its powers, and to its duties; and, without such fidelity, there can be no safety. It is, in all cases, the first and final and only judge of the qualifications, elections, and returns of its members; and so long as it holds that power in its right hand, and exercises it discreetly, firmly, fearlessly, we need have no fear of the Executive.

The same gentleman suggests, that this was not a free election, because the persons who voted at the election voted for the purpose of avoiding the effects of the proclamation of the President of the United States; or, as the proclamation of the military governor somewhat curiously terms it, to avail themselves of the "benefits" secured by the proclamation; to wit, the benefits of holding men in bondage. I beg leave to call the attention of gentlemen to the fact, that the proclamation of Sept. 22 nowhere holds out the hope of exemption from its operation to any district because it should have a member of Congress; that, on the other hand, the proclamation of Sept. 22 is put upon the distinct ground, that it is not a district, but the State, which is to be represented, and by an election at which a majority of the voters of a State voted. The suggestion in the proclamation of the governor was, therefore, without authority, unless derived from other source than the proclamation of Sept. 22.

But, if that proclamation had contained this promise in exact terms, I do not see why loyal and faithful people might not desire to avoid the practical effects upon them, whether legal or illegal, constitutional or in conflict with the Constitution, wise or unwise. That argument proves too much. It goes to this extent, that elections are not to be influenced by the consideration, that those engaged in them may thus secure more effectually the protection of the Government. One very excellent reason why they should exercise the elective franchise, and send members to this House, is to effect that object.

I put this case, then, upon two or three plain grounds. I put it upon the ground, that these men, who are asking seats in this House, are loyal citizens of the United States; that they have been elected by loyal citizens of the United States; that they have been elected at an election which was free; that they were elected by numbers, which, compared with other elections, indicate that the people in the districts were in the movement, and that it was had in entire good faith. I put it upon the plain ground, that while you demand of the loyal people of Louisiana faithful allegiance and obedience to your laws, and to bear the burdens of your Government, you should give to them the inestimable rights which that Government was formed to secure to them; without which they would be subjects, and not citizens; slaves, and not freemen. I put it upon the still higher ground, that the loyal men in the State of Louisiana, who have not engaged in this rebellion, or have returned at the earliest moment to their allegiance, have a right to come before you, and ask that you shall not permit the mere letter of the law, which to-day throws upon them all the weight and burdens of the Government, to stand in the way of the exercise of their dearest and most sacred rights, the rights which bind them to you, and make them of you.

Mr. Speaker, permit me to make one other practical suggestion to the House; and that is, that the only way in which you can reconstruct this Government is by the co-operation of the loyal men in the seceded States. If you mean to go a step further, and try to bring these States under absolute subjection, wipe them out of existence, and reconstruct them according to your will and pleasure and not their rights, you have taken upon yourself a task which you have not the power to execute, and which, if you had, would result in the overthrow of your liberties as well as theirs. No government would be a fit instrument for such a work but a military despotism. History gives us no hope in such a war. But if, on the other hand, you expect, as it seems to me every rational man must expect, to reconstruct the Government with the sympathy, co-operation, and aid of the loyal men of these States, then I ask you, in the name of prudence and of justice, not to shut the doors of this House against them. Do not, I beseech you, teach them the terrible lesson, that your powers are effective to destroy, but not to redeem; to crush, but not to save. Meet them at the threshold; welcome and bless them as they seek once more the shelter of the old homestead.

CONSCRIPTION BILL.

HOUSE OF REPRESENTATIVES, FEB. 25, 1863.

The House resumed, as the regular order of business, the consideration of the bill of the Senate (No. 511) for enrolling and calling out the national forces, and for other purposes.

Mr. THOMAS obtained the floor.

The SPEAKER. The gentleman from New York having already spoken, and not being the mover or introducer of the proposition, cannot speak again without the leave of the House. The gentleman from Massachusetts [Mr. Thomas] is entitled to the floor.

Mr. BAKER. Will the gentleman from Massachusetts yield to me for a moment?

Mr. THOMAS, No, sir: I cannot yield for any purpose. I have but twenty minutes.

Mr. HOLMAN. I rise to a point of order. I sought the floor at the time the gentleman from New York [Mr. Olin] did, and raised upon him the point of order which has been disposed of by the Chair; and I think, therefore, I am entitled to the floor.

The SPEAKER. The Chair did not understand the gentleman from Indiana as claiming the floor, but only as raising the question of order. If the gentleman raised it desiring to speak himself, he is entitled to the floor.

Mr. HOLMAN. I understand that the gentleman from Kentucky [Mr. Crittenden] and the gentleman from Massachusetts [Mr. Thomas] desire to be heard on this bill, and I am unwilling to occupy the time of the House while those gentlemen desire to speak. I will, therefore, yield to those gentlemen; and I now resign the floor to the gentleman from Massachusetts.

Mr. THOMAS. Mr. Speaker, I thank my friend from Indiana [Mr. Holman] for his great courtesy in yielding to me the floor. I rejoice, with exceeding joy, that I have no party interests to represent, no party topics to discuss. I have heard with sorrow, not to say disgust, the voices of discord and bitter strife from both sides of the House. If the spirit of party cannot be subdued or chastened in the presence of our imminent peril, God save the country; for he only can.

In the few remarks I shall have time to submit to the House, I would look directly to the merits of the measure before us. Mr. Speaker, this is a terrible bill; terrible in the powers it confers upon the Executive, terrible in the duty and burden it imposes upon the citizen. I meet the suggestion by one as obvious and as cogent; and that is, that the exigency is a terrible one, and calls for the use of all the powers with which the Government is invested.

Some of the features of the bill my judgment condemns, unhesitatingly condemns.

The period for which the service is required is unreasonably long. I think the enrolment should not include judges of the State courts, or ministers of the gospel, or members of Congress of either branch; though the inclusion of members of Congress would be, I think, simply void. I earnestly object also to the provision of the bill for the arrest of civilians by the military power; but I understand that gentlemen upon my right will consent to an amendment which shall strike out that feature. But, saving these objections, I think the bill is within the scope of the Constitution, and necessary and just.

First, the question of *power*. Congress has power to "declare war." A necessary incident to this power would be that of raising and supporting armies. But the power to "raise and support armies" is given in terms. No limitation is imposed as to the numbers to be raised, or the mode of raising. In the nature of things, such limitation could not be imposed. The power must be broad enough to meet all possible exigencies; and the possible exigencies of the country no man or prophet could foresee. The powers of Congress within their scope are supreme, and strike directly to the subject, and hold him in their firm and iron grasp. I stand by the opinion, early expressed upon this floor, that there is not a human being, domiciled within the territory of the United States, black or white, bond or free, whom the Government may not use for its military service, whenever the defence of the country requires; and of this exigency Congress alone must judge.

Is the exercise of the power to raise armies made dependent upon the consent of the individual citizen? I say, clearly not. "Government is not *influence*," said Washington; it is not moral suasion. That only is government which can command obedience and enforce it. The duty of the citizen to defend the State is admitted. Does the discharge of that duty depend upon his will and discretion, or the will and discretion of the Government? If upon the former, the objection is fatal even to any militia law: if upon the latter, the extent, and mode of use, are questions for Congress only.

The question was asked half a century ago, whether, under the power to support armies, Government could take property without consent; and, if not, how it was, that, under the power to raise armies, you can take men without consent. I answer, that very clearly, for the support of the war, you may take the property of the subject without his consent, but not without compensation; for the fifth article of the Amendments has put this limitation upon your power.

Under the "Articles of Confederation," Congress had not power to raise armies, though it had to build and equip a navy. Its duty was to agree upon the number of land forces, and to make requisitions upon each State for its quota (Art. 9). But the men who framed the Constitution, knew, by the experience of the Revolution, how defective and inadequate was such power, and that, whatever possible danger there might be in the grant of the power without limitation, any limitation might prove fatal to the national defence. The power was therefore given to raise armies without qualification; and, though the subject of much bitter complaint and criticism in the State Conventions, to-day at least its necessity is plain to all men.

Having the power to raise and support armies, and

the exigency existing in which the use of that power is necessary, the question arises, whether the powers given to Congress and the States, with respect to the militia, qualify and restrain the power to raise and support armies. Very clearly not, Mr. Speaker. They are distinct, independent powers. The militia is a branch of service well understood in the mother-country and our own, to be called forth " to execute the laws, suppress insurrections, and repel invasions." It was not designed for permanent service, but to meet special exigencies, and for brief periods of time.

Much has been said, though without much reflection, about the very " unpatriotic " course of the Government of Massachusetts with respect to the use of the militia in the war of 1812. The opinion of the Supreme Court of Massachusetts of that day proceeded, as I recollect it, upon the ground, that, the purposes of the militia being to suppress insurrection and repel invasion, the militia of the State could not be required by the Federal Executive to go beyond the limits of the State. To that view I do not assent; but it is, I think, quite plain, they are not, in the light of the Constitution, a part of the army of the United States: they are to be enrolled and organized for the purposes stated in the Constitution, and for no other.

This unqualified power to raise and support armies is given us to meet an hour and an exigency like this.

The gentleman from Kentucky [Mr. Wickliffe] says that the army is made up, and has been made up, by volunteer enlistments, and that you never have " conscripted" men into the army. Doubtless, such has heretofore been the practice; but the exigency never before arose when it was necessary to conscript men into an army. The exigency does not confer new powers, but evokes them into service. At this moment, the question, whether we shall use this power, is not one of expediency merely; not what is best. It is, in effect, a question, to this nation, of life or death. We literally have no choice.

Gentlemen upon my right (the Republican side of the House) know that it is my conviction, that all the vaunted panaceas for our troubles have failed, utterly failed. I expected them to fail. I attempted in vain to satisfy the House, that it was leaning upon reeds shaken by the wind. My earnest, repeated suggestions were, of course, unheeded; but the results are too palpable to be overlooked or mistaken, and reason is slowly re-ascending the steps of its throne. Pray God it may not be too late.

The policy inaugurated on the 1st of December, 1861, has been fruitless of good: it has changed the ostensible, if not real, issue of the war. That policy, and the want of persistent vigor in our military counsels, render any further reliance upon voluntary enlistments futile. The nostrums have all failed. Confiscation, emancipation by Congress, emancipation by the proclamation of the President, compensated emancipation, arbitrary arrests, paper made legal tender, negro armies, will not do the mighty work. Nothing will save us now but vicrories in the field and on the sea; and then the proffer of the olive branch, with the most liberal terms of reconciliation and re-union. We can get armies in no other way but by measures substantially those in the bill before us, unless the Administration will retrace its steps, and return to the way of the Constitution, for us the strait and narrow way which leads unto life. The war on paper is at an end. The people have, for a time, been deluded by it. That delusion exists no longer. If you are to suppress this Rebellion, all instrumentalities will fail you but the power of your own right arm.

Mr. Speaker, the measures and policy heretofore pursued have not been merely fruitless of good; they have been fruitful of evil: they have made, or largely contributed to make, a united South; they have made a divided North; they have alienated from the Administration the confidence and affection of large portions of the people; they have paralyzed your arm, and divided your counsels. Gentlemen flatter themselves this alienation and disaffection are the work of the Democrats; that the people have been misled and deceived by their wiles. Sir, the people of this country read, and keep their eyes open, and comprehend; and the plain fact is, you cannot unite them upon the policy you now pursue. They do not believe in destroying the Union and Constitution in the hope of building up better by force of arms. You may unite them on the issue of maintaining the Union and the Government at every price and cost, but upon no other.

Having distracted the public mind, having alienated to a great degree the affection and confidence of the country, what is left to you? To resort to those constitutional powers vested in you for the preservation of the Government which you have in trust, and which you must use, or be false to that trust. Gentlemen say the people will not bear this measure. I will not believe it. I believe the people of this country are ready to do and to endure every thing for the preservation of their unity, their national life, and, through that unity and that national life, all that makes life precious to men: they will submit to it. In view of the infinite interests at stake in this great controversy; in the solemn conviction that there is to-day no hope of peace except in disintegration; that, as a nation, we must conquer in arms, or perish; they will meet and respond to this imperative call of duty. Such is my hope and trust.

But, Mr. Speaker, suppose they hesitate; suppose they do not submit: you can but try; you have no other hope. The negro will not save you; paper money will not save you; your infractions of personal liberty will not save you. If the illegal and unnecessary arrests are persisted in, in the peaceful and loyal States, they will ruin you. Go firmly to the people, and present to them the real issue: they will understand the terrible exigency in which the country is placed; and they will be true to that country, if you show clearly to their comprehension the length and breadth and height and depth of that exigency. Mr. Speaker, the issue must be met at all hazards. If the people will not support you, if they will not do this highest act of duty, the days of this Republic are numbered, the end is nigh. Satisfy them that you mean to be true to the Constitution and the Union, and they will be true to you, and will uphold and save you.

The issue, I repeat, must be met. You die *without* this measure: you can no more *with* it, except you die, as cowards die, many times. I go, therefore, for appealing from panaceas and make-shifts to this highest, most solemn, and imperative duty of the citizen to protect the life of the State.

NEW ENGLAND AND THE UNION.

HOUSE OF REPRESENTATIVES, FEB. 28, 1863.

Mr. SPEAKER, — The most careless observer of the signs of the times will not have failed to notice the attacks, frequent, persistent, ubiquitous, upon the history, character, and policy of New England. The evidence of union and concert in these attacks is plain; and, what is very significant, the concert includes the politicians and presses of the States in arms against us. The aim and purpose of these attacks are palpable. They are not for counsel, rebuke, chastening: to these we might give heed for possible good. The obvious purpose of this war of words is to create a feeling of bitter hostility to New England in the Western and Middle States (the traitors in arms against the Union hate her now with sufficient intensity); to force the conviction upon those States, that the character and policy of New England are such, that the good-will and harmony of the country cannot be maintained while she forms part of the Union; and to bring about a reconstruction on the basis of the Confederate Government, slavery for its corner-stone, and "New England left out in the cold."

The element of the New-England character and policy, which, it is averred, makes union with her intolerable and impracticable, is her Puritanism. In an age of discoveries, that discovery is the most remarkable. After Puritanism has been upon the continent two centuries and a half, building up free institutions; after union with it for three generations, its light following the light of the sun, and kindling the western horizon with new glory; after having suffered and toiled with it, and been inspired by it through the Revolution; after having enjoyed with it, or in spite of it, for seventy-four years, the freest and most beneficent Government the Divine Ruler ever permitted to man; the country learns, with surprise, it has all the while been under the saddest of delusions; that what it had fondly believed a "spirit of health," is, in truth, a "goblin damned;" that New England is a diseased limb of our body politic, that must be severed, or the whole body perish.

With scarcely less surprise, if at a time like this we have a right to be surprised at any thing, do we observe by whom these assaults upon New England are made. By those who claim to be the especial friends of the democratic institutions which Puritan hands planted and Puritan tears watered in the wilderness of the New World. By the especial friends of personal liberty, of which, under the Tudors and Stuarts, the Puritans were the depositaries; and of which, from that day to this, they have been the vigilant and zealous defenders. By the especial friends of the Union, which germinated on the New-England soil, and of which the humble confederation of the New-England Colonies was the forerunner and the prophecy. By the especial friends of the Constitution, which, in the hour of its past perils, has found in New-England statesmen some of its firmest bulwarks, and, in the greatest of them all, its great defender. With Virginia, who, by her resolutions of 1798, inserted the wedge, which, from that day, she has driven deeper and nearer to the heart of the Union; with South Carolina, which, more than thirty years ago, set up the standard of revolt, and has been laboring for a generation, with persistent malignity and folly, to destroy the Government she had felt only in its blessings; with the Gulf States, who are seeking, by a rebellion remorseless and bloody, to plunge themselves and the country into the gulf of woe and perdition; with these, Union is possible and desirable, but not with the Puritans of New England!

Leave them to perish on their granite, ice-bound peaks! Theirs is a restless spirit, the very genius of discontent. They disturbed the repose of the Tudors; they reformed the Reformation; they took from one Stuart his head, and from another his throne; they secured Magna Carta; they gave to civil liberty the Petition of Right; they left merry England in the hey-day of its material prosperity, where, could they have appreciated the tranquillity of despotism, they might have laughed and grown fat; they left the homes of childhood, the graves of fathers, and faced ocean, wilderness, want, the savage foe, merely to pray as the spirit taught them to pray. *Simple* men, they might have worshipped God in solemn temples, in cathedral aisles, the eye ravished with beauty, and the ear with music. They sought rather the rude log-house in the forest, or the temple not made with hands; preferring to royal favor the favor of the King of kings. They planted their humble commonwealths upon a sterile soil and in an inhospitable climate. Their institutions were laid on the rough granite of English liberty. Instead of seeking to bask in royal sunshine, they stood out in the cold, and contrived to bar their doors, not only against intruders, but against the king. Loyal to the crown when the crown let them alone, they maintained, from the beginning, a substantial, sturdy independence. When separation came, it is among the most striking things in history to observe how slight changes in the framework of government were necessary. For ninety years, Mr. Speaker, their destinies have been blended with those of the other colonies. From many States sprung up one nation. To-day, New England finds upon her soil more than three millions of free, intelligent, happy people. A million of living men born upon that soil have their homes in the other States. One-third of the population of the United States is of New-England descent; its ancestral graves and memories with us.

The Puritans have borne with them toward the setting sun the institutions, the manners, the culture of New England; the meeting-house, the town-house, the common school, the college, the village library. They were not without the weaknesses and follies of their time, and follies their own; but in spite of these, and over and above these, they had the elements of character which fit men to be the founders of empire, — *conditores imperiorum*, — firmness, courage, prophetic sagacity, serene, unfaltering trust in God. And they were the founders of an empire; a beneficent, a glorious, let us pray the infinite Lawgiver, an enduring empire.

But I forget, Mr. Speaker: wise men have discovered not only that the sun has spots, but that it is the spots that make up the sun; and that, after all, there is no light or life or healing in his beams; that the clothes are more than the man, the outward more than the inward, the accidental and temporary more than the vital and permanent. The history of three centuries is to be rewritten; the judgment of the civilized world to be reversed; the House of Stuart to be recanonized; the locks of the Cavalier to be recurled, and the Roundhead again set upon the stocks for the rabble to pelt. The task is formidable; but as wit has a keen edge, and error and calumny are swift of foot, it may be well to notice briefly some items of the great debt we owe to the Puritans and their descendants, and some of the grounds of attack.

The debt which *personal liberty* owes to the Puritans can scarcely be overstated. By liberty I mean no philosophical abstractions, no platitudes of French philosophy, but practical, personal freedom, intrenched in, and defined and upheld by, sovereign law; the sense and right of security which makes a man's house his castle, and his person sacred; a man's right to life, property, the use of his brain and of his lips, within the pale of the law, and unless deprived of them by due process of law; the right without which all the forms and machinery of free government are mockery, delusion, and fraud. It is to the Puritans of the time of Charles I. we owe the great Petition of Right, to whose lofty yet eminently practical ideas of liberty our times have not climbed.

Let me ask the Clerk to read the passages I have marked. Observe, Mr. Speaker, how history repeats itself. " I praised the dead who are already dead more than the living who are yet alive."

"Whereas also, by the statute called the Great Charter of the liberties of England, it is declared and enacted, that no freeman may be taken or imprisoned, or be disseized of his freehold or liberties or his free customs, or be outlawed or exiled, or in any manner destroyed, but by the lawful judgment of his peers, or by the law of the land;

"And, in the eight and twentieth year of the reign of King Edward III., it was declared and enacted, by authority of Parliament, that no man, of what estate or condition that he be, should be put out of his land or tenement, nor taken nor imprisoned nor disinherited, nor put to death, without being brought to answer by due process of law;

"Nevertheless, against the tenor of the said statutes, and other the good laws and statutes of your realm to that end provided, divers of your subjects have of late been imprisoned without any cause showed; and when, for their deliverance, they were brought before justice by your majesty's writs of *habeas corpus*, there to undergo and receive as the court should order, and their keepers commanded to certify the causes of their detainer, no cause was certified but that they were detained by your majesty's special command, signified by the lords of your Privy Council, and yet were returned back to several prisons, without being charged with any thing to which they might make answer according to the law;

"And whereas also, by the said Great Charter, and other of the laws and statutes of this your realm, no man ought to be adjudged to death but by the laws established in this your realm, either by the customs of the same realm or by acts of Parliament; and whereas no offender, of what kind soever, is exempted from the proceedings to be used, and punishments to be inflicted, by the laws and statutes of this your realm; nevertheless, of late time, divers commissions, under your majesty's great seal, have issued forth, by which certain persons have been assigned and appointed commissioners, with power and authority to proceed within the land, according to the justice of martial law, against such soldiers or marines, or other dissolute persons joining with them, as should commit any murder, robbery, felony, mutiny, or other outrage or misdemeanor whatever, and by such summary course and order as is agreeable to martial law, and as is used in armies in time of war, to proceed to the trial and condemnation of such offenders, and them to cause to be executed and put to death according to the law-martial:

"By pretext whereof, some of your majesty's subjects have been, by some of the said commissioners, put to death, when and where, *if by the laws and statutes of the land they had deserved death, by the same laws and statutes also they might, and by no other ought to, have been judged and executed.*"

You will not fail to observe, Mr. Speaker, that there is no complaint that the writs of *habeas corpus* were not issued. They were issued, and the subjects brought before justice, and the keepers commanded to certify the cause of their detainer. The ground of complaint is, that no cause was certified, but that the subjects were *detained by his majesty's special command, and were returned to prison without being charged with any thing to which they might make answer according to the law.* The "privilege of the writ" was suspended. This is all that can be done, under the Constitution, by Congress or the Executive, or both combined.

Again: observe the lofty moral ground a Puritan Parliament assumes. It concedes that the persons against whom the "justice of martial law" has been used might be "dissolute, and such as should commit murder, robbery, felony, mutiny, and other outrages and misdemeanors;" but it never occurred to the great authors of this Petition that men *charged* with crimes "had no rights." They knew, as we know, that when men were the objects of hatred or suspicion, it was then, and chiefly then, they needed the shield and protection of standing laws.

The Puritan Parliament goes on to pray (demand) that the commission for proceeding " by martial law" may be revoked, and that thereafter no commissions of a like nature may issue. To which, in full Parliament, the king answered, "Soit droit comme il est désirée."

I regret my time will not permit us to hear every word of this gospel of personal liberty. If the Puritans had given us nothing more, our debt of gratitude could never be paid. The writ of *habeas corpus* of Charles II. did not enlarge these liberties. It was remedial only. As such, it was highly beneficial; but it conferred no new right. "Its office," says Hallam, "was to cut off the abuses by which the Government's lust of power, and the servile subtilty of crown lawyers, had impaired so fundamental a privilege."

If we cross the ocean with the Pilgrims, we shall find them not only affirming, but strengthening, the muniments of personal liberty. Proof of this may be found in the " Body of Liberties" enacted by the Colony of Massachusetts in 1641. (I hope I shall be pardoned for taking Massachusetts, the mother-colony, as an illustration.) Let me, Mr. Speaker, have two or three of these " Liberties" read, to show their general temper and spirit, and how grossly the colonists have been misunderstood: —

" The free fruition of such liberties, immunities, and privileges as humanity, civility, and Christianity call for as due to every man in his place and proportion, without impeachment and infringement, hath ever been, and ever will be, the tranquillity and stability of churches and commonwealths; and the denial or deprival thereof, the disturbance, if not the ruin, of both."

In God's name, amen! Heart and head say, amen!

"No man's life shall be taken away; no man's honor or good name shall be stained; *no man's person shall be arrested, restrained, banished, dismembered, nor any ways punished;* no man shall be deprived of his wife or children; no man's goods or estate shall be taken away from him, nor any way endangered, under color of law, or countenance of authority, *unless it be by virtue or equity of some express law of the country warranting the same,* established by a General Court, and sufficiently published, or, in case of the defect of a law in any particular case, by the word of God; and in capital cases, or in cases concerning dismembering or banishment, according to that word to be judged by the General Court."

Magna Carta planted on the soil of the New World.

"Every man, whether inhabitant or foreigner, free or not free, shall have liberty to come to any public court, council, or town-meeting; and, either by speech or writing, to move any lawful, seasonable, and material question, or to present any necessary motion, complaint, petition, bill, or information, whereof that meeting hath proper cognizance, so it be done in convenient time, due order, and respective [respectful] manner."

Was ever the sacred right of petition made so practical and effective?

"No man's person shall be restrained or imprisoned by any authority whatsoever before the law hath sentenced him thereto, if he can put in sufficient security, bail, or mainprise for his appearance, and good behavior in the mean time, unless it be in crimes capital, and contempts in open court, and in such cases where some express act of court doth allow it.

"Every man that is to answer for any criminal cause, whether he be in prison or under bail, his cause shall be heard and determined at the next court that hath proper cognizance thereof, and may be done without prejudice of justice.

"No church censure shall degrade or depose any man from any civil dignity, office, or authority he shall have in the Commonwealth.

"We likewise give full power and liberty, to any person that shall at any time be denied or deprived of any of these liberties, to commence and prosecute their suit, complaint, or action, against every man that shall so do, in any court that hath proper cognizance or judicature thereof."

These humble colonists comprehended that there could be no justice which was not remedial; or where the way to redress was blocked at every step.

Now, I do not contend, Mr. Speaker, that the founders of New England were always true to their own professions, always realized their own ideal. Far from it: they had not only the infirmities of the race, but the superstitions and weaknesses of their time; when the powers of light were in struggle with those of darkness, and held divided empire. This I claim for them, that they apprehended the dawning light, and wove its golden threads into the texture of their political fabric. Theirs was the toil of the distaff: ours, the robe of light.

"Be to their faults a little blind;
Be to their virtues very kind."

The founders, and four generations of their descendants, have passed away. Massachusetts, having renounced her allegiance to the British Crown, and in the midst of a terrible struggle to make good the declaration, repairs the framework of her government. The people will have a broad, comprehensive declaration of rights precede the first grant of power. Opening with the averment, that all men are born free and equal; with the recognition of their duty to worship God, and of the right to worship him according to the dictates of conscience; that government is instituted for the people, and all its just powers derived from them; this declaration proceeds to define and secure the rights of personal liberty. The Constitution of Massachusetts makes it the duty of her public servants frequently to recur to and faithfully to observe these principles. At the risk of tasking your patience, I will recur to and read a few of the more vital. They are the beacon-lights of our history. Let us pray the time may not come when they shall serve only as monuments and memorials of a better age.

"Every subject of the Commonwealth *ought to find a certain remedy, by having recourse to the laws, for all injuries or wrongs which he may receive in his person, property, or character.*

"No person shall be arrested, imprisoned, or despoiled, or deprived of his property, immunities, or privileges, put out of the protection of the law, exiled, or deprived of his life, liberty, or estate, but by the judgment of his peers or the law of the land.

"Every person has a right to be secure from all unreasonable searches and *seizures of his person, his houses, his papers,* and all his possessions. All warrants, therefore, are contrary to this right, *if the cause or foundation of them be not previously supported by oath or affirmation.*

"The liberty of the press is essential to security of freedom in a State: it ought not, therefore, to be restrained in this Commonwealth.

"*The military power shall always be held in exact subordination to the civil authority, and be governed by it.*

"The power of suspending the laws, or the execution of the laws, *ought not to be exercised but by the Legislature, or by authority derived from it;* to be exercised in such particular cases only as the Legislature shall expressly provide for.

"No person can, *in any case, be subject to law-martial, or to any penalties or pains by virtue of that law,* except those engaged in the army or navy, and except the militia in actual service, *but by authority of the Legislature.*"

Mr. Speaker, these principles have been instilled into me from childhood. I drank them in with my mother's milk. They come to me crowned with precious ancestral memories. They are bone of my bone, flesh of my flesh, of the very warp and woof of my being. They define for me the word "liberty," the bright particular jewel of which the forms of free government are but the setting. I can understand the change in the setting: I cannot understand the crushing of the jewel. These principles have been my counsellors here: I have walked in their path; I have been guided by their light. My sense of what fidelity to them required has compelled me to dissent from some of the measures of the Administration; nay, more, earnestly to oppose them. I have regretted the occasion, but have had no question as to my duty; and, without a shadow of fear or distrust, I abide, the hour of excitement and passion past, the sober judgment of the Commonwealth of my love and pride. God bless her, whether she condemn or uphold!

To return. When, eight years later, the question as to the adoption of the Constitution of the United States was presented to the people of Massachusetts, they objected that no Bill of Rights was made part of the nation's supreme law. They led the way in the adoption of the amendments which make up our national Magna Carta. Articles two, three, six, seven, and ten, are from the Massachusetts Bill of Rights. Articles one, four, five, and eight, are found in our Bill of Rights, but were substantially taken from the Declaration of Rights of Virginia in 1776.

These facts show the traditional, settled policy of

Massachusetts. Her personal-liberty bills had their origin in this her lifelong devotion to this policy; in the desire of her people to give to the humblest man on her soil, to the fugitive from bondage, the presumptions of the common law, and *habeas corpus*, and trial by jury. I do not say, her legislation did not overstep the just boundary between the powers of the State and National Governments: I think it did. But, having had occasion to examine carefully that legislation, I do say, that its character has been grossly misrepresented. I do aver, that in no respect in which that legislation passed a hair's-breadth the line of State powers has it been sustained by the judiciary of the State. I do say, that there never has been a day or hour, when the arrest of any fugitive from service has been defeated by any statute of Massachusetts recognized and enforced by its judicial tribunals. I do aver, that by no law or judicial decree in that Commonwealth have the rights of any one master, in any one case, been destroyed or impaired. I always opposed that legislation, because I felt it was incapable of doing any legal, substantial good, and was not, in spirit, loyal to the Union; because it wounded and grieved the friends of the Union. The traitors who brooded over and gave life and form to this Rebellion knew full well that their rights had never been impaired by these laws; and were driven to the shallow pretence, that the void act of a State Legislature, not upheld by its courts or executive, had the effect to nullify acts of Congress, and prevent their execution. See the ordinance of secession of South Carolina; false premises leading to false conclusions.

A people willing to risk so much to guard the rights of the fugitive from service cannot fail to view with deep sensibility the arrests made in the peaceful and loyal States, where no plea of necessity now obtains, whose usual channels of justice are unobstructed, in violation of the muniments of liberty, to illustrate and secure which has been their glory and pride. They cannot but regard with distrust, if not with indignation, the subtile lawyer and the time-serving politician, who not only defend, but stimulate and encourage them. They cannot but deprecate the recurrence of acts which serve only to weaken the love of Union, and to encourage and give comfort to its foes.

Let us turn now, for a moment, to the debt which *The Union* owes to New England. As I have before suggested, the germ of the Union is to be found in the confederation of the New-England Colonies in 1643, with its Union army of two hundred and thirty-five men. In the articles of this confederation may be found the great idea and thought, embodied and made effective in the Constitution, the reconciliation of central power with local independence; for security against dangers without, and conflicts within, mutual protection and reciprocal dependence; for domestic institutions and local interests, independence and entire self-control. The distribution of powers between the central Government and the States, and the States and the municipalities, is the great political thought which we have organized and illustrated; unity without centralization, unity with diversities of policy and operation. The result of unity with centralization would be despotism, whatever the outward form: the fruit of unity with diversity has been the most beautiful illustration the world has seen of the largest liberty blended with the firmest order. This humble confederation formed the first American Union, and contained the first fugitive-slave law.

If we come down to the Revolution, the labors and sacrifices of the New-England Colonies are matters of the most familiar history. Their present is trembling in the balance; their future is with God; their past has stood before the judgment-seat, and has put on the white robe. Rich as the country may be with glorious memories, she cannot part with these. The heavens may burn with other celestial lights; the mariner will not spare the north star. The New-England Colonies inaugurated the Revolution. The first blood was spilt upon their soil. The four New-England Colonies, with a population not exceeding nine hundred thousand, furnished to the war (in continental troops and militia) over one hundred and forty-seven thousand men. With one-third of the population of the United Colonies, they furnished two-thirds of all the troops; Massachusetts raising some twelve thousand more than the six Southern States. This is said in no spirit of boasting, Mr. Speaker; but, when our lot and right in the homestead are questioned, it is not ungraceful to allude to our labors in securing it.

To the administration and policy of Washington, New England was a firm and unwavering friend. For sixty years, her politics, with slight departures, were of his school. Need I say, that, if the policy and counsels of the Father of his Country had been followed by the whole country, this terrible civil war would have been averted; that, since the resolutions of 1798, we have increased the centrifugal forces of the Government, instead of the centripetal; have thought too much of the States, and too little of " that unity of government which constitutes us one people "?

There was a brief time, indeed, when New England, her commerce paralyzed, her industry prostrated, by the policy of the National Government, seemed to be starting from her sphere; but she soon easily and naturally resumed her wonted orbit of order, law, and obedience. From the peace of 1815 to 1850, faithful to the Constitution and the Union, she advocated broad and national views of the Constitution, and a liberal use of the powers of the General Government for the development of the industry and material resources of the country.

New England is often reproached on this floor for the Tariff policy of the Government. She did not inaugurate the policy. It was not her choice. When the country embarked in it, and the industry and capital of New England had been diverted to manufactures, she felt, and justly, that they had a claim to the continued care and protection of the Government. At no time since the inauguration of this policy has she controlled the counsels of the Administration; and, for the greater part of the time, she has had a limited influence in those counsels. She has, indeed, believed that such an adjustment of duties on imports as would protect our industry was just and wise and beneficent for all parts of the country; but, for the inaugurating and establishing the tariff policy, she may not claim the credit, and is not responsible.

The charge against New England, of a *narrow and illiberal policy towards the West*, is also without the least foundation in fact. In his great speech in reply to Mr. Hayne, in 1830, Mr. Webster indignantly repelled the charge, then first conjured up, for narrow party purposes:

"I deny that the East has at any time shown an illiberal policy towards the West. I pronounce the whole accusation to be without the least foundation in any facts existing either now or at any previous time. I deny it in the general, and I deny each and all its particulars. I deny the sum total, and I deny the detail. I deny that the East has ever manifested hostility to the West, and I deny that she has adopted any policy that would naturally have led her to such a course."

With respect to the *distribution of the public lands*, the Governor of Massachusetts, and one of her wisest sons (John Davis), in 1841, in a special message to the Legislature, declared "that the new States were entitled to a more liberal share of the public lands than the old States, as we owe to their enterprise much of the value the property has acquired." And a resolution was passed by the Legislature, declaring,

"That, in the disposition of the public lands, this Commonwealth approves of making liberal provisions for the new States; and that she ever has been, and still is, ready to co-operate with other portions of the Union in securing to these States such provisions."

Equally just and liberal has been the course of New England in relation *to the system of internal improvements in the new States*. Said Mr. Webster, in the speech before referred to,

"I assert, boldly, that in all measures conducive to the welfare of the West, since my acquaintance here, no part of the country has manifested a more liberal policy. I beg to say, sir, that I do not state this with a view of claiming for her any special regard on that account. Not at all. She does not place her support of measures on the ground of favor conferred. Far otherwise. What she has done has been consonant to her view of the general good, and therefore she has done it. She has sought to make no gain of it: on the contrary, individuals may have felt, undoubtedly, some natural regret at finding the relative importance of their own States diminished by the growth of the West. New England has regarded that as the natural course of things, and has never complained of it. Let me see any one measure favorable to the West which has been opposed by New England, since the Government bestowed its attention on these western improvements. Select what you will, if it be a measure of acknowledged utility, I answer for it, it will be found that not only were New-England votes cast for it, but New-England votes secured its passage."

That her course since 1830 has been equally just and liberal, the records of both Houses of Congress attest.

For the great system of internal improvements, the result of private enterprise, by which the Valley of the Mississippi has been brought so near to us, and its vast material resources so marvellously and rapidly developed, the West is to a very large extent indebted to the capital and enterprise of New England. Capital was doubtless seeking a profitable investment; but the investments would not have been made but for the large reciprocal trust and confidence between New England and the West.

Five hundred million dollars, a liberal share of the amount from New England, have been expended in the canals and railroads constructed to give to the great lakes a new outlet to the sea. The great consumers of the products of the free States in this valley are northeast of it. Forty-nine fiftieths of the cereals of the North-west, seeking a foreign market, find their way, by these new channels of communication, to the tide-waters at New York. The real mouths of the Mississippi open to the North-east. Art, labor, and the iron will of man, are stronger than Nature, and mould and bend her to their purposes. Ties of birth, kindred, marriage, early associations, memories of fatherland, common institutions, common culture, thought, faith, reciprocal and interdependent interests, bind the North and West together. Crafty and selfish politicians cannot sever them. They *can* sever from themselves the affection and confidence of the people of both sections. *They can leave themselves out in the cold.*

Such, Mr. Speaker, briefly, hastily stated, were the principles and traditional policy of New England to the close of the first half of the present century.

I do not shrink from the consideration of her position and relations to the Union for the last twelve years, or her position to-day. I must speak freely, and with the love that casteth out fear. I am not insensible of the power which radical, not to say disorganizing, revolutionary views have acquired among us; the setting-up of private speculations and feeling under the guise of " higher law," and party formulas and dogmas above the obligations of duty and the mandates of the supreme law of the land.

There are, I know, men in New England who are opposed to the existing Union, to " any union with slave States." They control, to some extent, the political machinery of the States. They are the channels through which the honors and patronage of the National Government are chiefly distributed. They are men of talent, culture, ubiquity, and intense activity; an activity and ubiquity that supply the place of numbers. Some of our pulpits and presses catch and reflect the glow of their fiery zeal. These, Mr. Speaker, are not Puritans, nor the children of the Puritans. They have wandered from the fold and faith of their fathers. Government, to them, has no root in the divine will or counsels. They know not, they cannot understand, *the liberty of obedience.* They do not recognize the truth, that the powers that be are ordained of God. Some of them have substituted a diluted Platonism, or German pantheism, for the gospel of Jesus Christ, and mutual admiration for the worship of Almighty God. But *these* do not represent the mind or heart of New England, its material or moral forces. This condition of things with us is not more the fruit of the activity of the radical, than of the supineness and neglect of duty of the conservative men of New England. *They* have been warned of the coming perils, and have either failed to foresee and gauge them, or have shrunk from the conflicts necessary to avert them. We cannot now escape without much tribulation and suffering; nor is it just that we should. We hold our institutions at a price we would not pay; sleepless vigilance. We were not faithful to our sacred trusts: we permitted visionary theorists, sectional partisans, fire-eaters, and radicals, North and South, to administer a government founded in concession, conciliation and compromise; and which we knew, or ought to have known, could never be upheld and maintained in any other spirit than that in which it was founded. These men had power to raise the storm: they have no pilot to weather it. The ship is drifting, no firm hand at the helm, between anarchy and despotism. Oh for the master-spirit to say to the waves, "Peace, be still!"

Mr. Speaker, the people of New England are, for the most part, a law-loving, a law-abiding people. They love liberty; but they know it can be had only in obedience to law, obedience of those who make and those who execute the laws. They have the largest possible stake in the present Union of the States. They do not, cannot fail to see, that, under any reconstruction of the Government, they have nothing to gain, every thing to lose. They will hear, reflect, give heed to the voice of reason and duty. They cannot be moved by scoffs and sneers; they cannot be driven. They make part of the Union. The largest sacrifices to win and secure it were those of their fathers. Its priceless blessings are theirs, in trust for their children. They will be faithful to that trust. The attempt from other States to exclude them from their inheritance would inaugurate a war, compared with which all we have seen of this would be but as ministrations of mercy. If those holding power in New England shall use it, or try to use it, to sever us from the Union, or to consent even to separation, they will hear in every city, town, and village, on every plain and hill-top, the cry which was rung out on the 19th of April, 1775, "To arms!" The men of New England have sworn, by the God of their fathers, that neither secession nor abolition shall rob them of their birthright.

Mr. Speaker, I have trespassed too long upon the

indulgence of the House, without having touched the grounds of attack upon the social and personal character of the Puritans and their descendants. It is scarcely necessary. "By their fruits ye shall know them. Do men gather grapes of thorns, or figs of thistles?" I will, however, glance at one or two points, which, my observation here has convinced me, have had their effect upon those who have not been with us, and are not familiar with our history.

Upon no point is attack more frequent, or error more prevalent, than upon the *social position, the culture and manners, of the Puritans.* The association of Puritanism with rudeness, and coarseness of taste and manners, has really no higher source than the doggerel of Butler, and the sneers of Hume and other apologists for the House of Stuart. In birth, culture, manners and wealth, the Puritans were among the best gentlemen of England. Need I recall to your recollection Hampden and Waller, the Earl of Essex, Manchester, Fairfax, Harry Vane, and John Milton, not less the world's greatest epic poet than the gentleman trained to all the graceful arts of his time? Need I remind you of the fact, that the aggregate wealth of the third House of Commons of Charles I., a Puritan House, was estimated to be three times that of the House of Lords? Need I refer you to the beautiful picture of a Puritan household in the Life of the young regicide, Colonel Hutchinson, by his accomplished and devoted wife? I may even suggest, that the sober garb of the Puritans has descended to the gentlemen of England, and the lace and embroidery to his servant. If you desire further to examine the subject (of little moment, I confess, in a country so democratic as ours), I invite you to read an admirable paper on this point in Sanford's "Studies of the Great Rebellion;" or the ninth chapter of the first volume of Palfrey's "History of New England;" a work worthy of its great theme.

Puritanism, like other movements political or religious, suffered from counterfeits. When its principles had triumphed, coarse, vulgar, greedy men assumed its garb, and debased and dishonored it; as men assume now devotion to the freedom of the slave, whose real devotion is to contracts for spavined horses and rotten vessels. Canters, self-seekers, wolves in sheep's clothing, men with long prayers and longer visages, followed in the path of Puritan victory to clutch its spoils. The true Puritan was sober, godly, self-denying; feeling he had a divine work to do, and doing it with his might. To say that he did not attain to his own ideal of duty, is to say that he was very like sensible and good men of later times of larger light and larger pretension.

Another alleged obnoxious trait of character of the Puritan (and his descendant) is his love of money, and craft in getting it. I meet the allegation at the threshold; I take issue on the fact; I utterly deny it. I have had opportunity to know something of the people of New England in the different callings and paths of life, and something of men on both sides of the water. I have studied men, with some diligence, in history. The New-Englander ("Yankee," if you please) loves to get money. He wants success in every thing to which he puts his hand; and he is very apt to succeed. He has thrift and providence. He lays by for the rainy day and shady slope of life. He abhors a vacant pocket, and the dependence which attends it; but, as a race, no men are more honest in getting money, or more liberal in the use of it, than the men of New England. Liberal in their own households, and in every work of kindness and Christian charity, no people live better, or give more freely; or understand better, that, to do either, a wise economy is necessary. Of course I am speaking of the general rule, which, like every rule, has its exceptions. Every soil has its crop of hucksters and petty craftsmen. Ours are peripatetic, and are very apt to emigrate South or West. Some find their way to Government agencies; and a few half way back,— to Washington.

The New-Englander is said also to be an intermeddler. How far, politically, he has concerned himself with the rights and interests of other portions of the country, I have had occasion briefly to suggest. Upon the matter of slavery, I cannot deny that a portion of our people have trespassed beyond the just bounds of State comity. But I cannot forget, that the bearing of the slaveholders toward the people of the North has naturally provoked hostility; and that from the sparks emitted in the collisions of extreme men, on either side, the fires of civil strife have been kindled. As an individual, the New-Englander has curiosity largely developed. He loves to know what is going on in the world. He is inquisitive; but these qualities are not peculiar to him. They were found in the first man and woman, and will be in the last. " But out of the rind of one apple tasted," said John Milton, "the knowledge of good and the knowledge of evil leaped forth into the world, as twins cleaving together." With all his interest to know what is going on in his neighborhood, he worships the god of boundaries, and will not remove the ancient landmarks. No man respects more constantly the division-line between his own and another's rights.

I conclude, Mr. Speaker, with a single suggestion. It is, that, under our system of Government (many States and one nation), differences of culture, manners, domestic institutions, of climate and its productions, and of forms of industry, may be reconciled, if there be the spirit of conciliation. Nay, more: experience is rapidly developing the truth, that in that diversity has been our security.

"All nature's difference makes all nature's peace."

Those differences all removed, the probable result would be the absorption of the powers of the States in the central Government, toward which our steps are tending. The States gone, or stripped of their most important functions, the central power, call it republic or by any other name you please, would be, in substance, a despotism.

THE END.

Printed in Dunstable, United Kingdom